In the Garden:
Book of Cartoons

Featuring Cartoons From
Narrative Magazine
The New Yorker
Weekly Humorist
and more!

Front Cover illustration: Jason Patterson
Back Cover illustration: Mort Gerberg
Introduction: Bob Mankoff
Design: Darren Kornblut
Layout: Adam Kornblut

Dedicated to Jennifer & Bea

Cartoon Collections, LLC
10 Grand Central, 29th Floor
New York, NY 10017

For cartoon licensing information visit www.CartoonStock.com
Create a personalized version of this book at www.CartoonStockGifts.com

First edition published 2024
Item # 46465
ISBN: 978-1-963079-00-5

Introduction

Ladies and gentlemen, garden enthusiasts and green-thumbed connoisseurs, welcome to a blooming marvelous collection of cartoons that celebrate the joys, quirks, and occasional frustrations of gardening! As the former Cartoon Editor of *The New Yorker*, I am delighted to present this delightful compendium where realm of horticulture meets the realm of humor.

Gardening, with its endless array of plants, pests, and possibilities, has always been a fertile ground for humor. It's a world where the beauty of flowers can be overshadowed by the audacity of weeds, where the serenity of a well-tended garden can be disrupted by the chaos of wildlife, and where the never-ending quest for the perfect bloom can lead to comical misadventures. Whether you're a seasoned gardener with years of experience or simply someone who enjoys a potted plant on their windowsill, these cartoons are sure to resonate with your green thumb and tickle your funny bone.

Our talented cartoonists have cultivated a diverse garden of humor. As you leaf through these pages, I hope you'll find not only laughter but also a deeper appreciation for the passion and dedication that go into tending a garden. Gardening is a labor of love, and sometimes, a little humor is just what we need to keep us going when the weeds seem relentless and the weather refuses to cooperate.

So, my fellow garden enthusiasts, dig in, leaf through these pages, and let the laughter bloom. This collection is a tribute to the green oasis we create in our lives, where nature and humor thrive side by side. Enjoy the whimsy, embrace the absurdity, and may your gardening adventures be forever fruitful and funny!

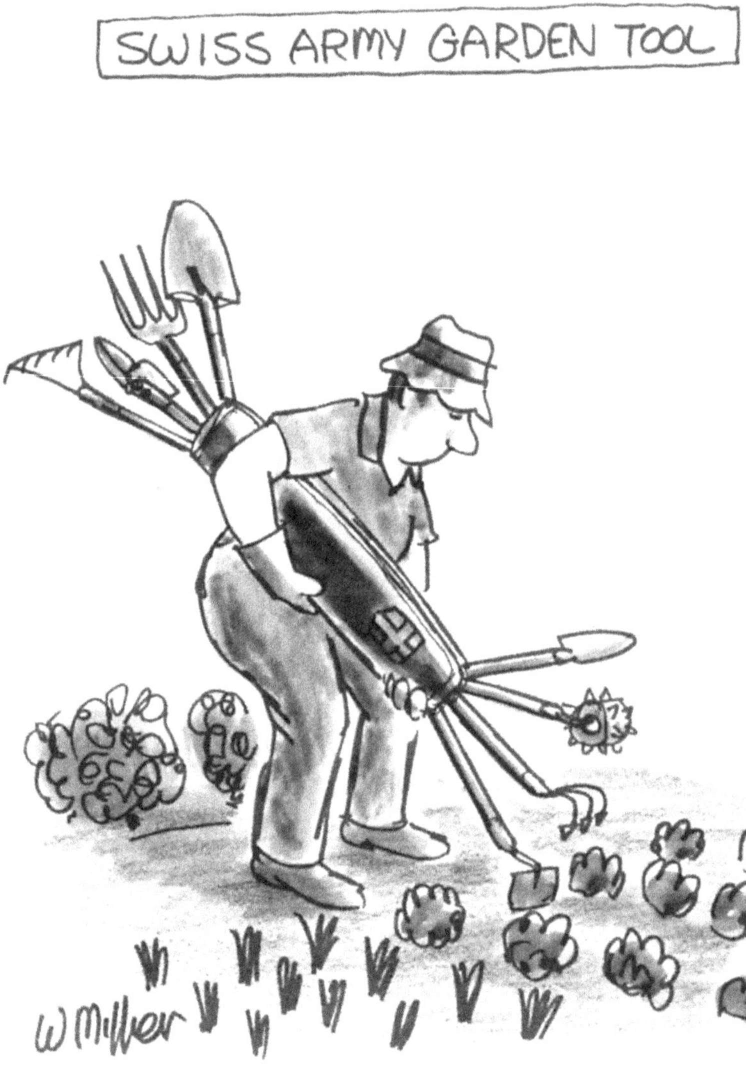
SWISS ARMY GARDEN TOOL
W Miller

JULY
BEGINNING
YARDER
$3.95
Say Hello to Grass!
What the Hell Is "Mulch"?
Rake or Hoe: Which Is Which?
No, You Don't Want a Pool
plus tons more!
SO, YOU'RE OUTSIDE. NOW WHAT?
pp. 3-8
R. Chast

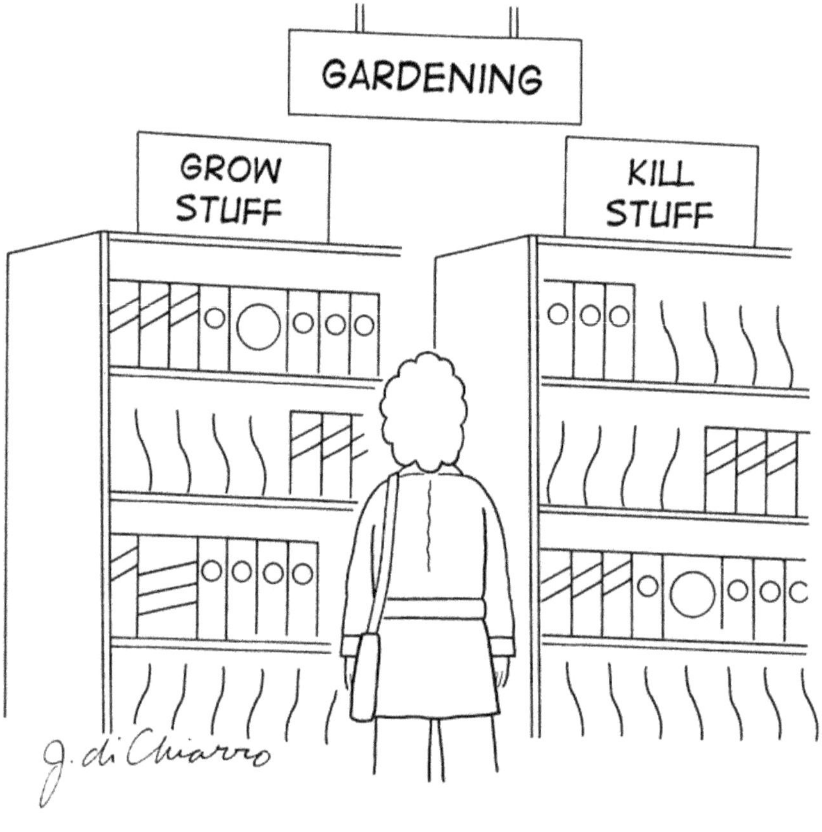
GARDENING
GROW STUFF
KILL STUFF
J. di Chiarro

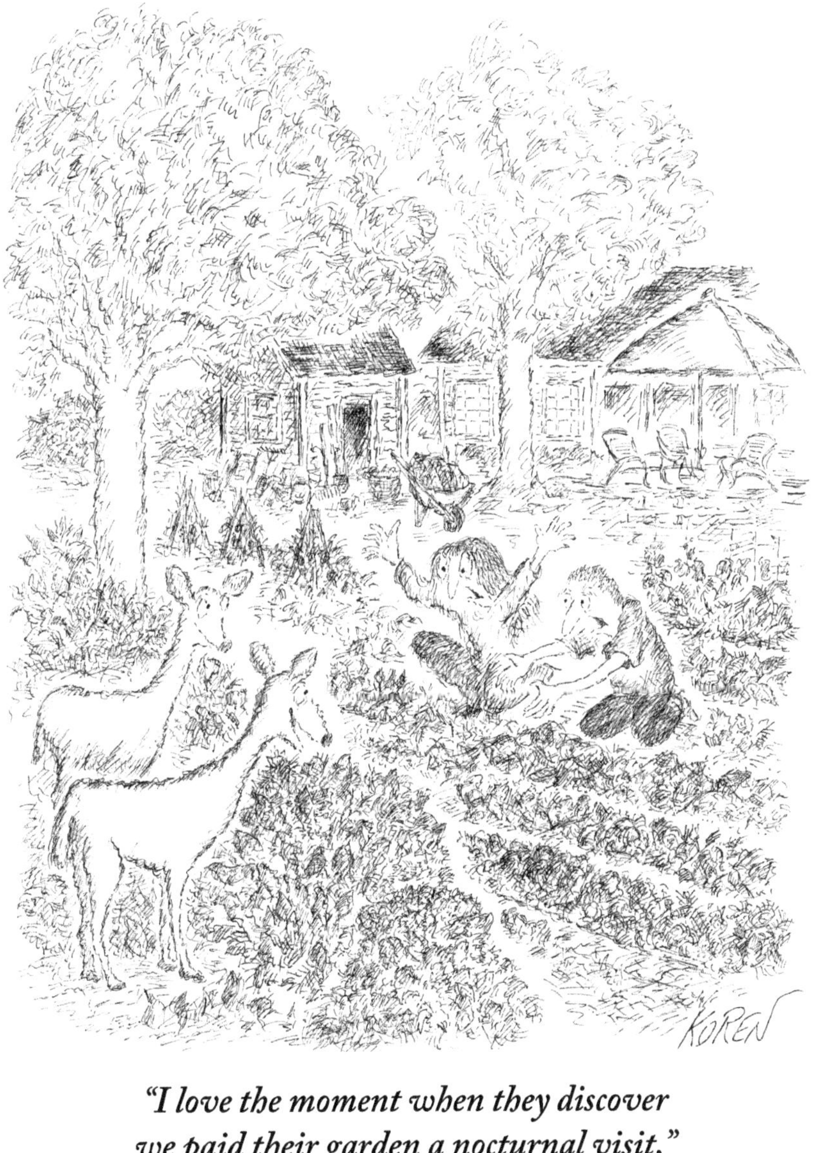
KOREN

"I love the moment when they discover we paid their garden a nocturnal visit."

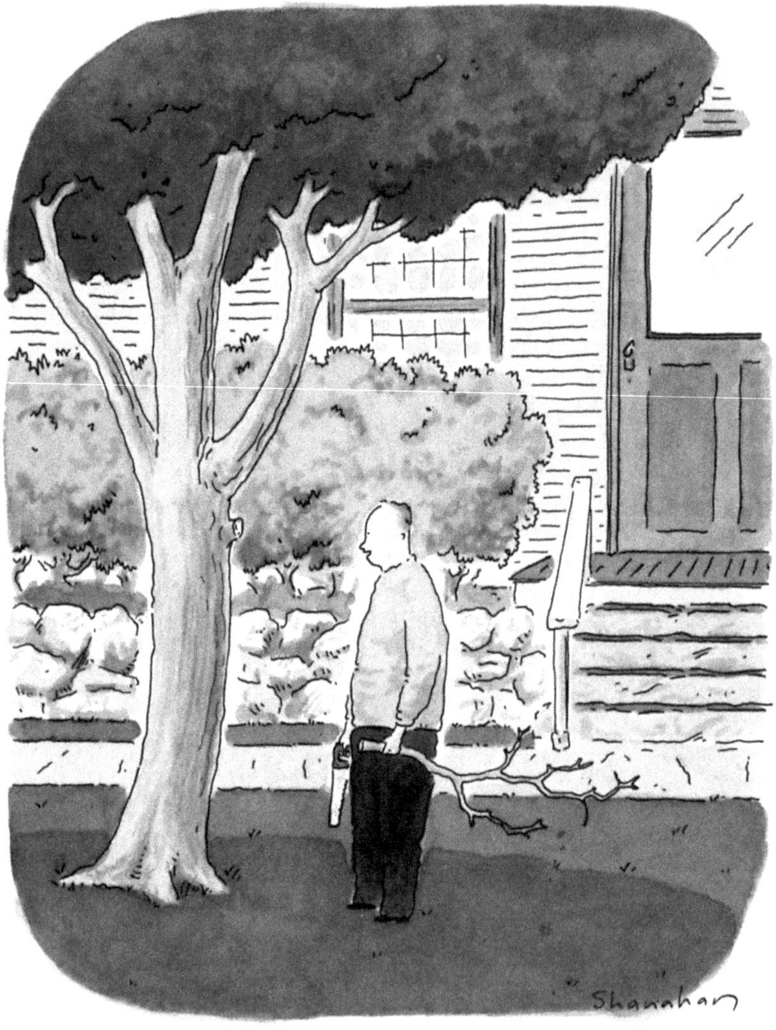
Shanahan

"You were very brave."

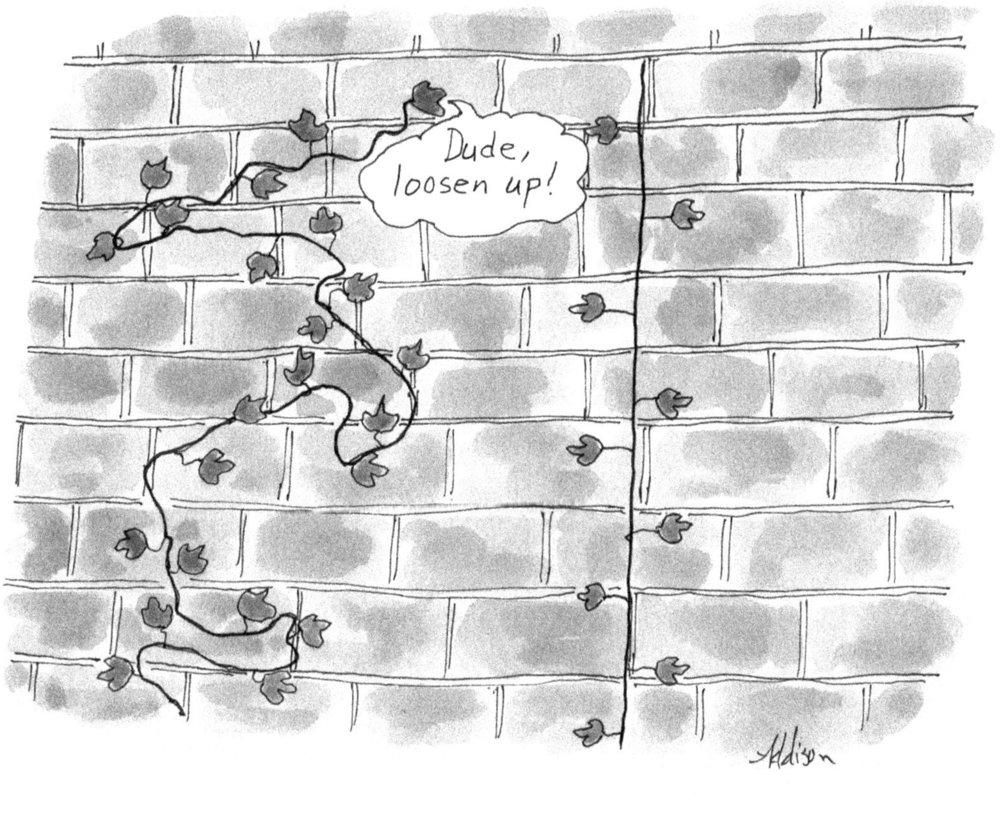
Dude, loosen up!
Addison

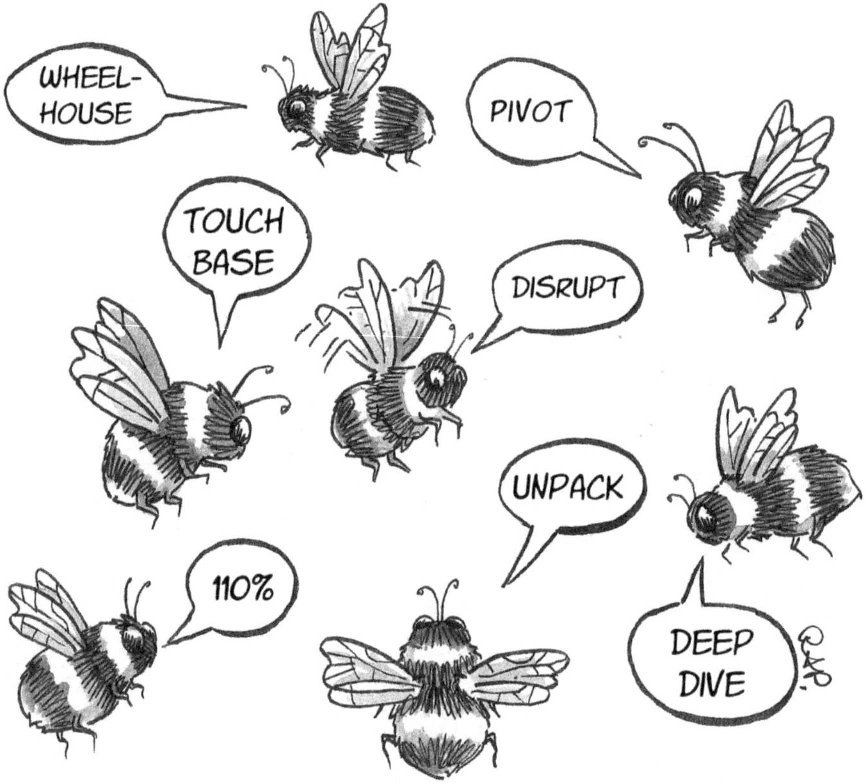
WHEEL-
HOUSE
PIVOT
TOUCH
BASE
DISRUPT
UNPACK
110%
DEEP
DIVE

Buzzwords

"*This one looks as though it could use a little nurturing.*"

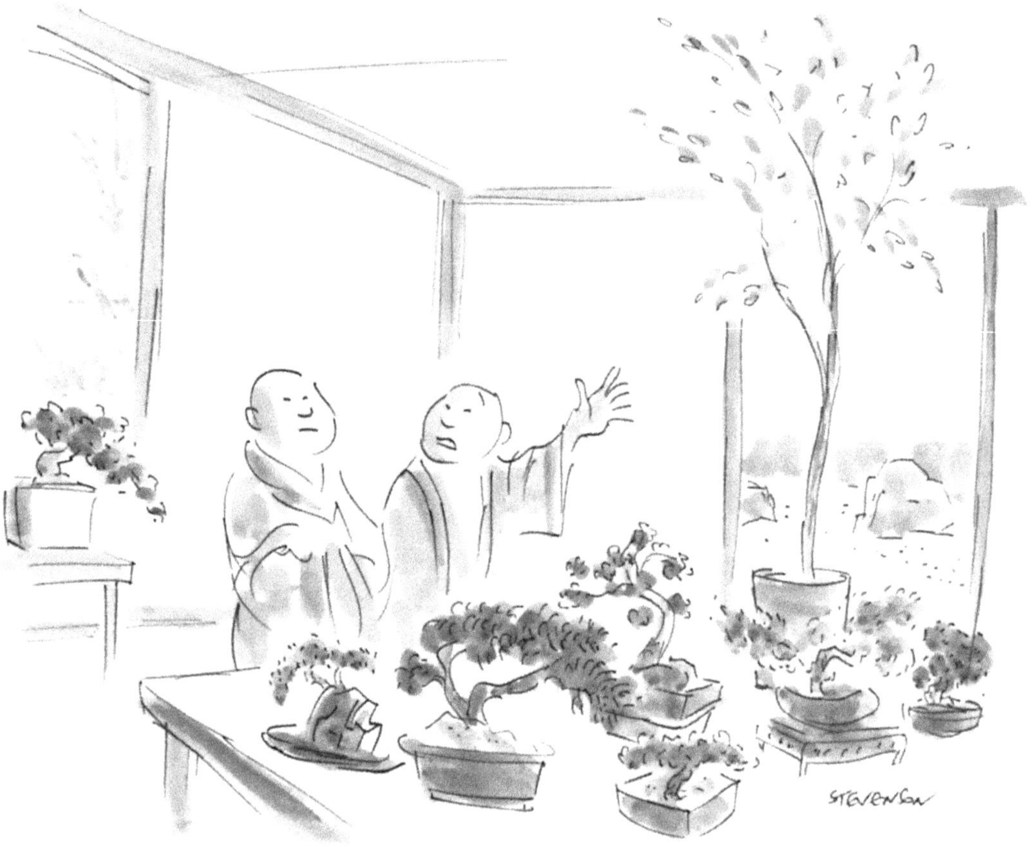
STEVENSON

"I don't know what went wrong."

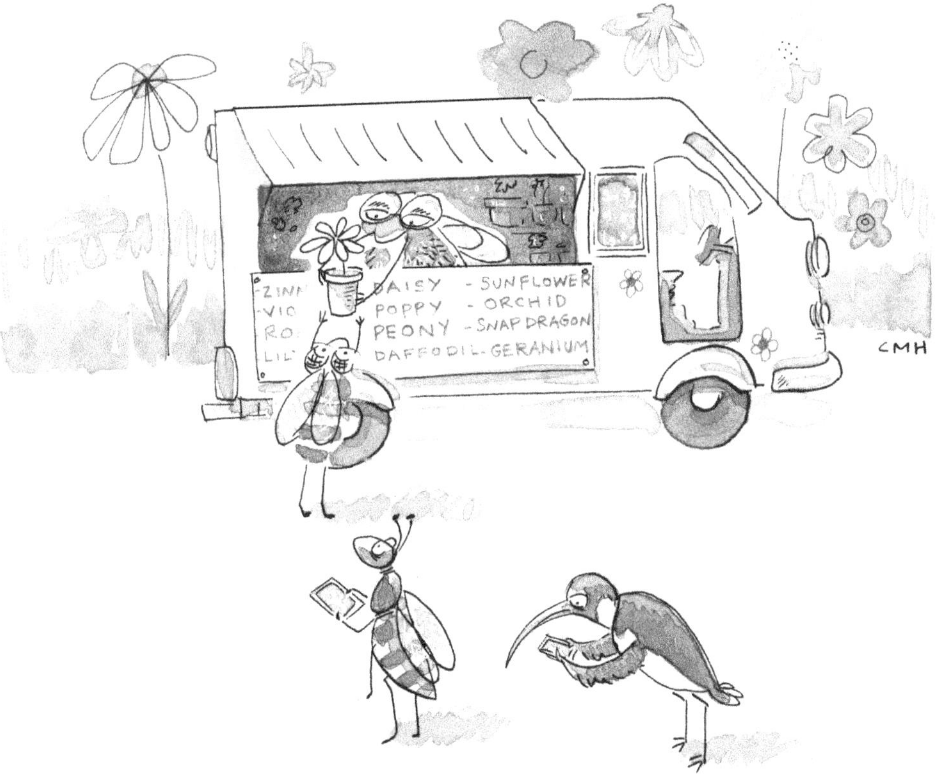
DAISY -SUNFLOWER
POPPY -ORCHID
PEONY -SNAPDRAGON
DAFFODIL-GERANIUM
CMH

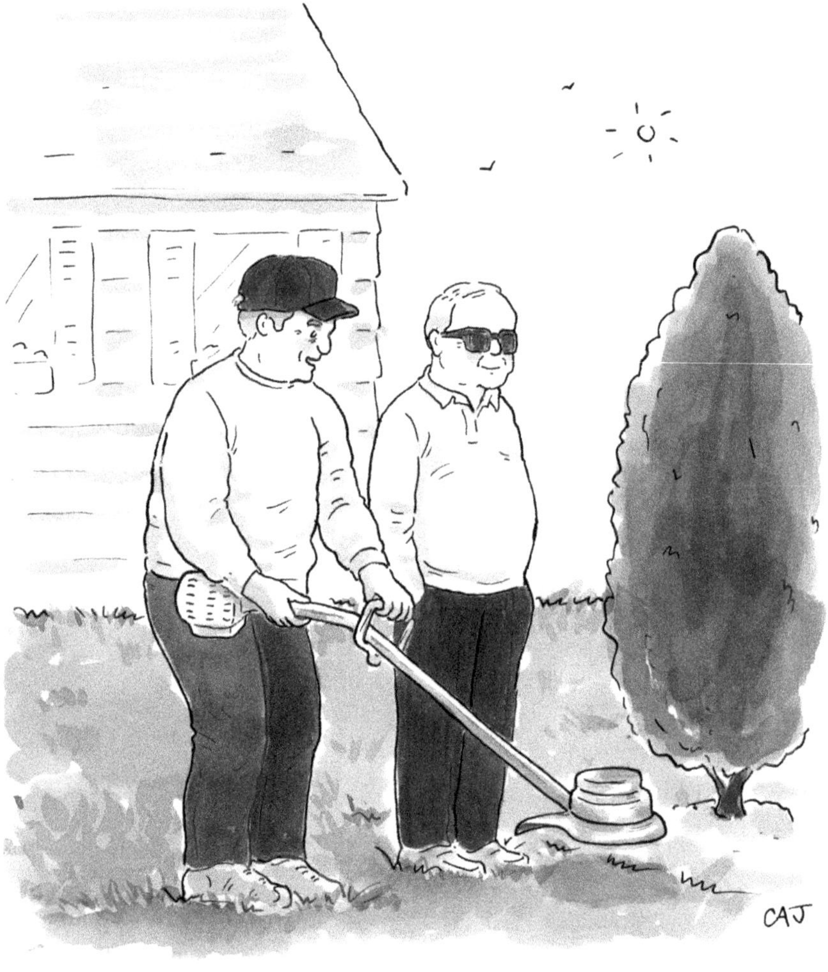
CAJ

"As weed-whackers go, it's a little quiet for my taste."

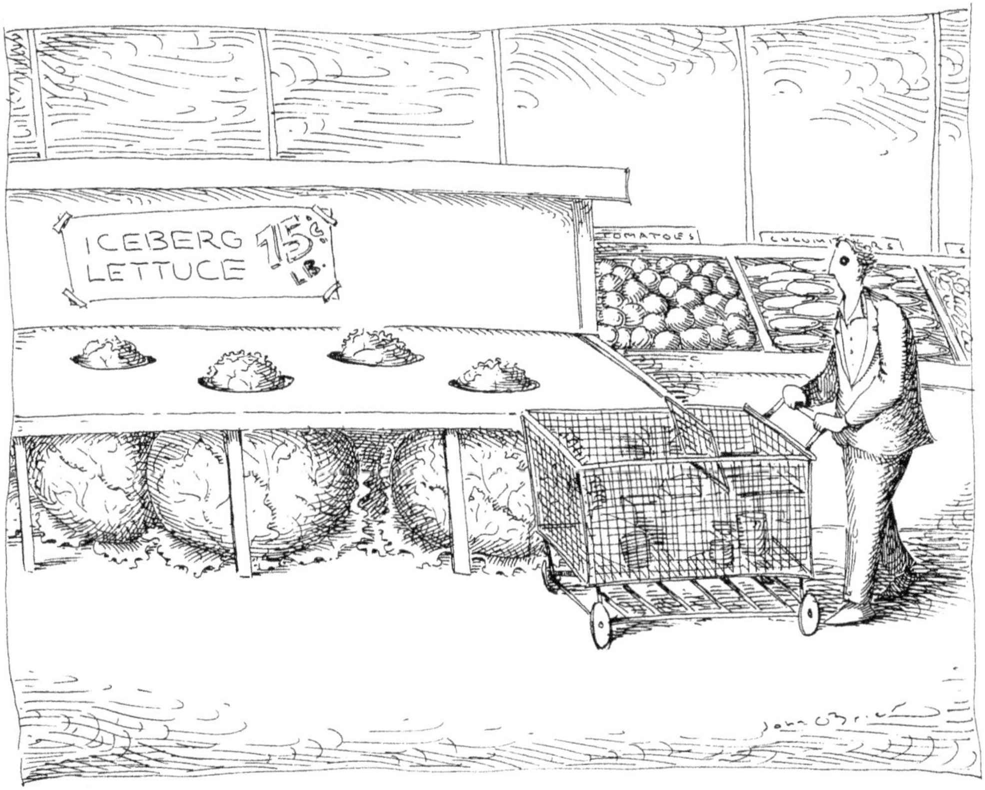
ICEBERG LETTUCE
15¢ LB.
TOMATOES

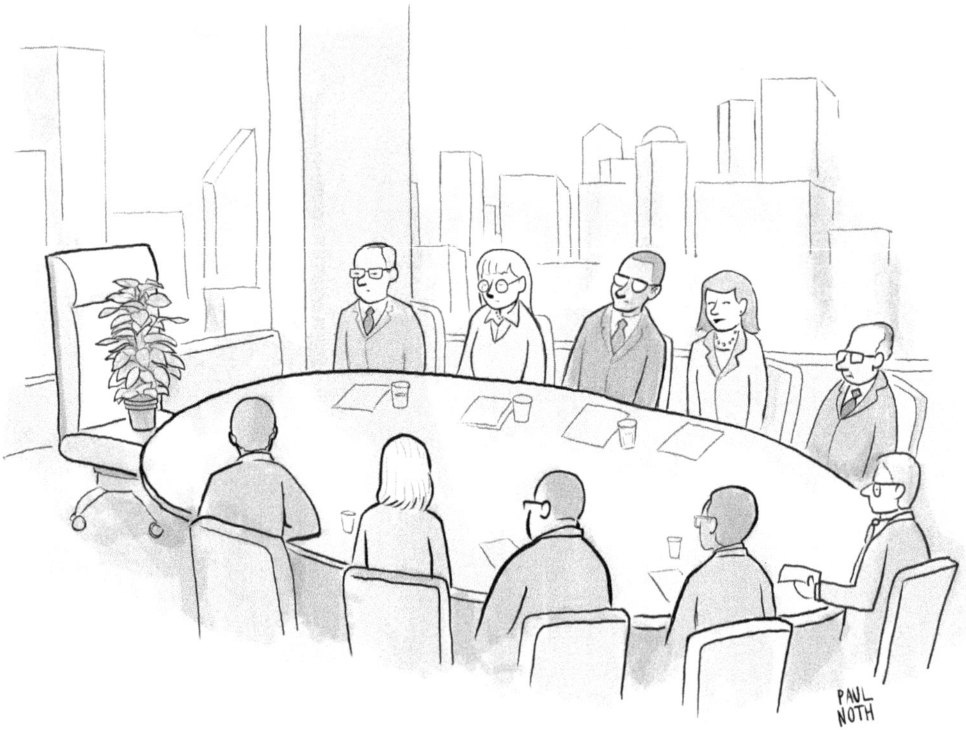
PAUL
NOTH

"It's amazing to think he started out in the lobby."

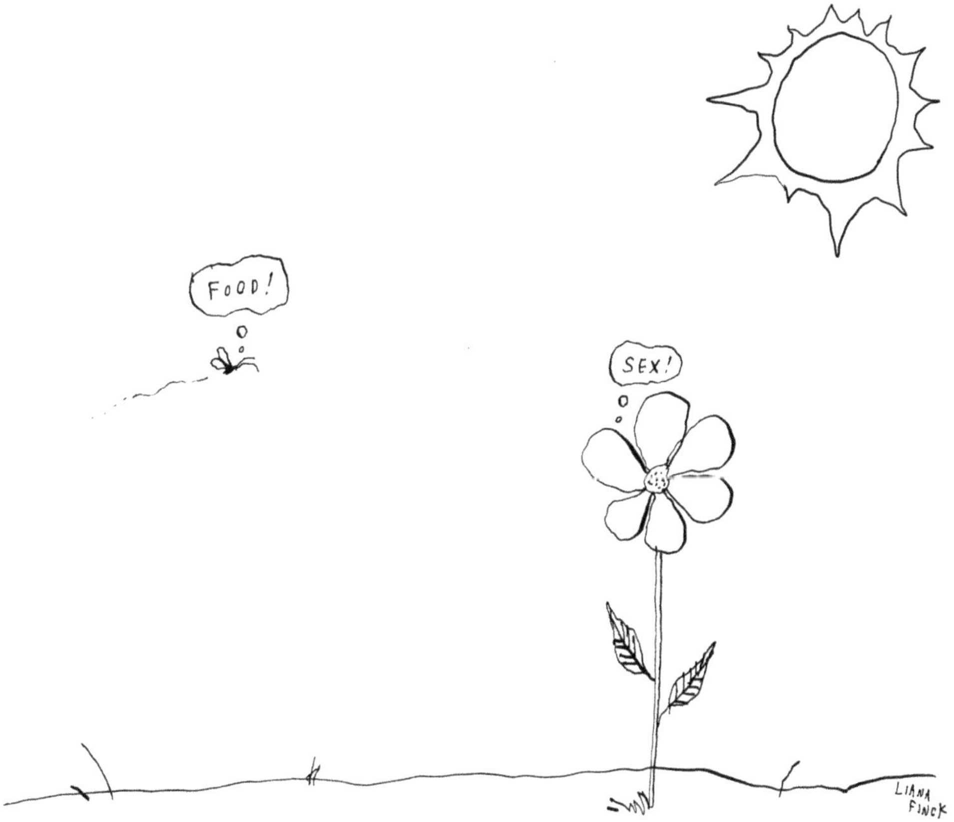
FOOD!
SEX!
LIANA FINCK

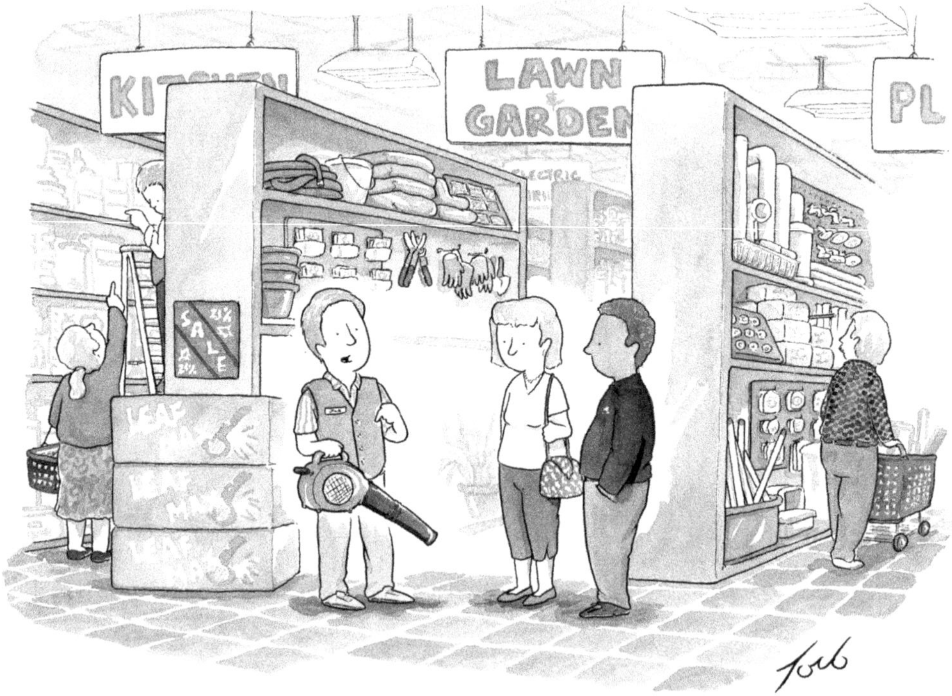
KI
LAWN
GARDE
PL
SALE

"When it comes to blowing leaves around uselessly and creating an insane amount of noise, this model can't be beat."

WEYANT

"It's the porch plants—an they come in?"

sdf

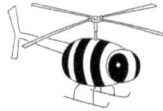

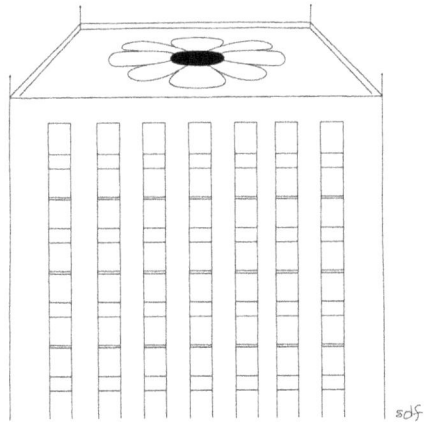

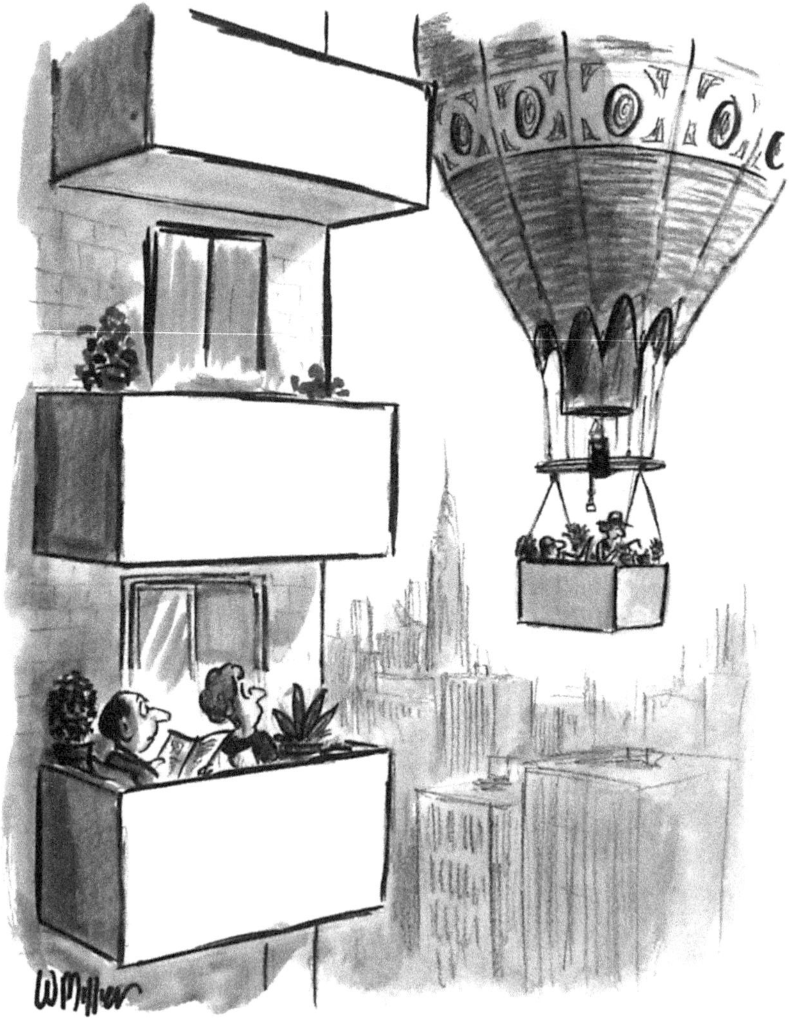
WMiller

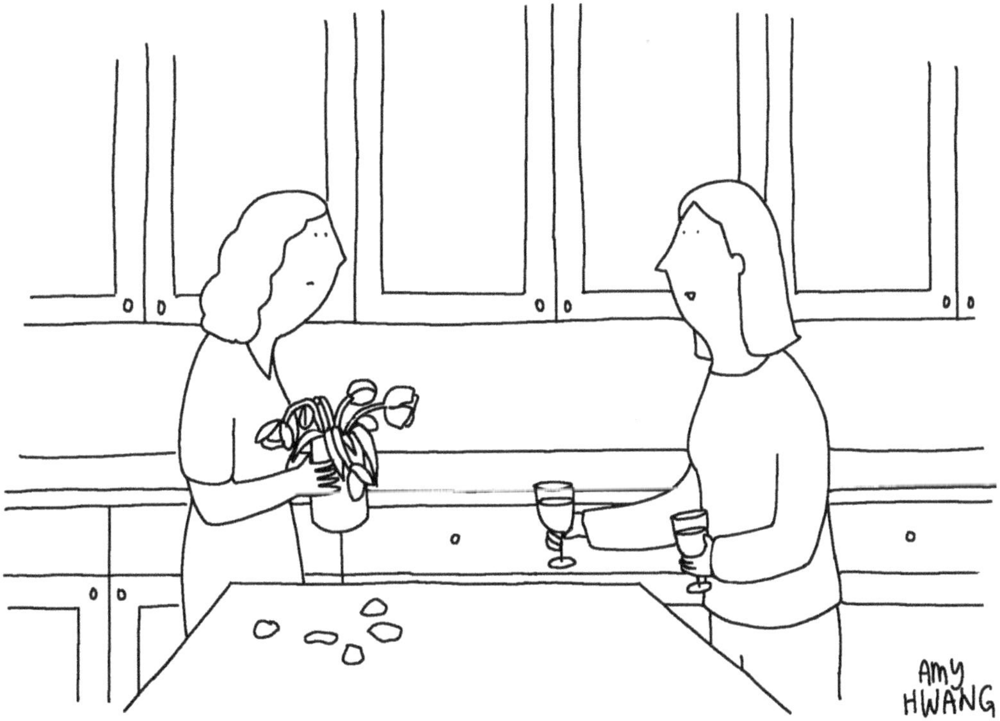
Amy
HWANG

"Don't worry. These roses are still fresh."

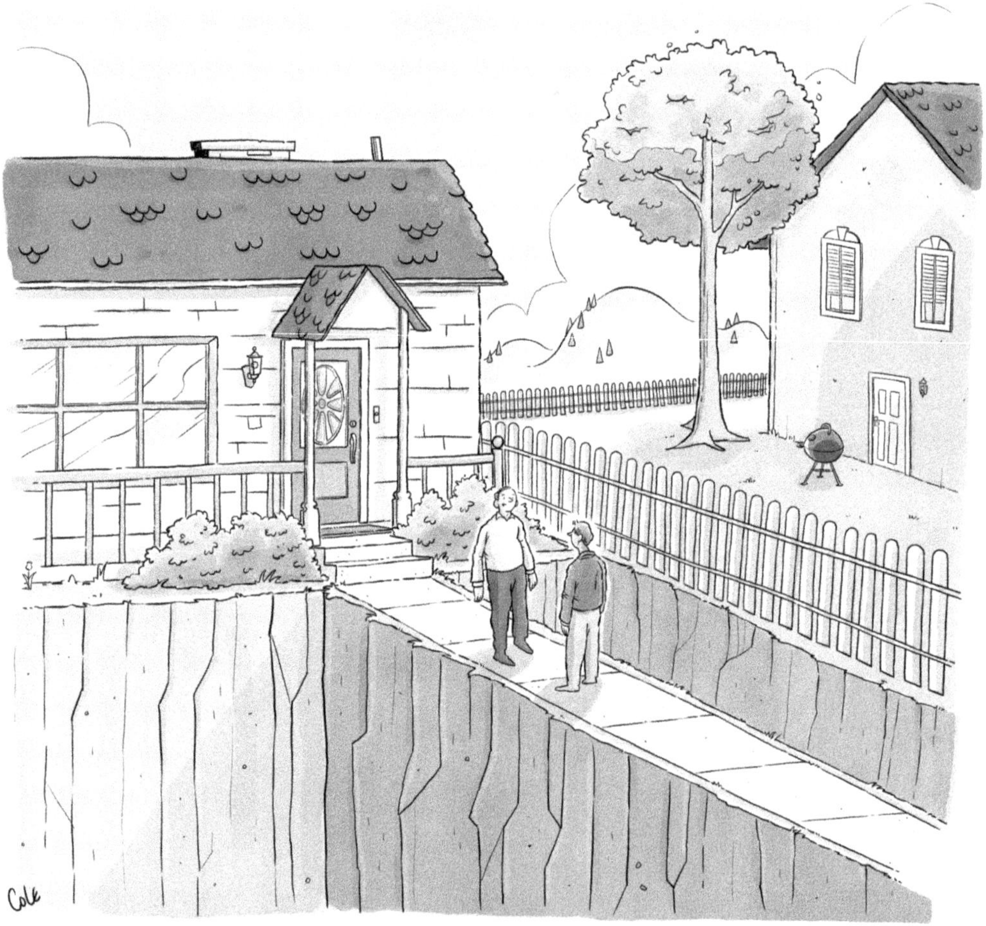
Cole

"I had a yard sale and somebody brought it."

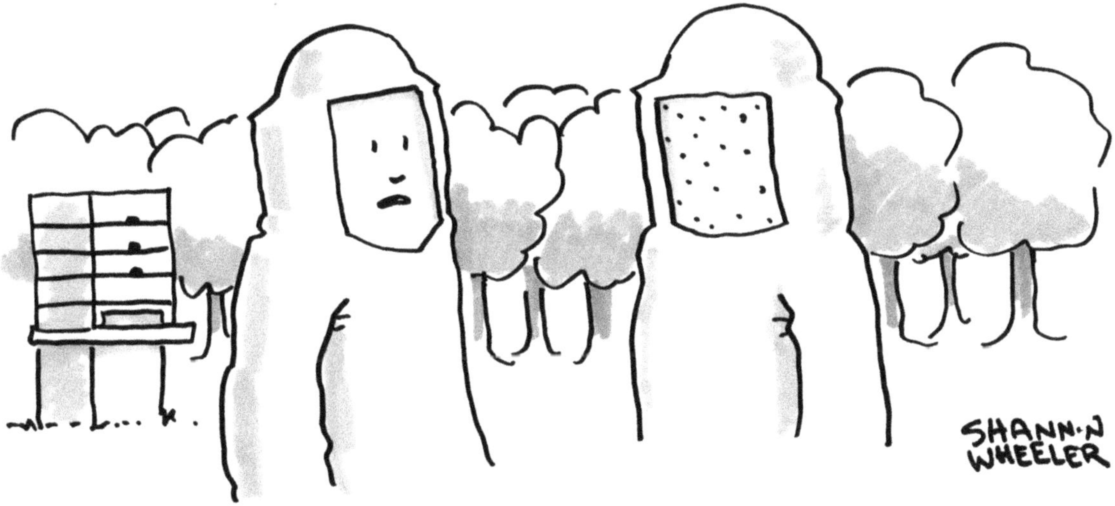
SHANN·N WHEELER

"John, the bees go on the outside."

TOMATOES
BROCCOLI
STRAWBERRIES
CORN
John O'Brien

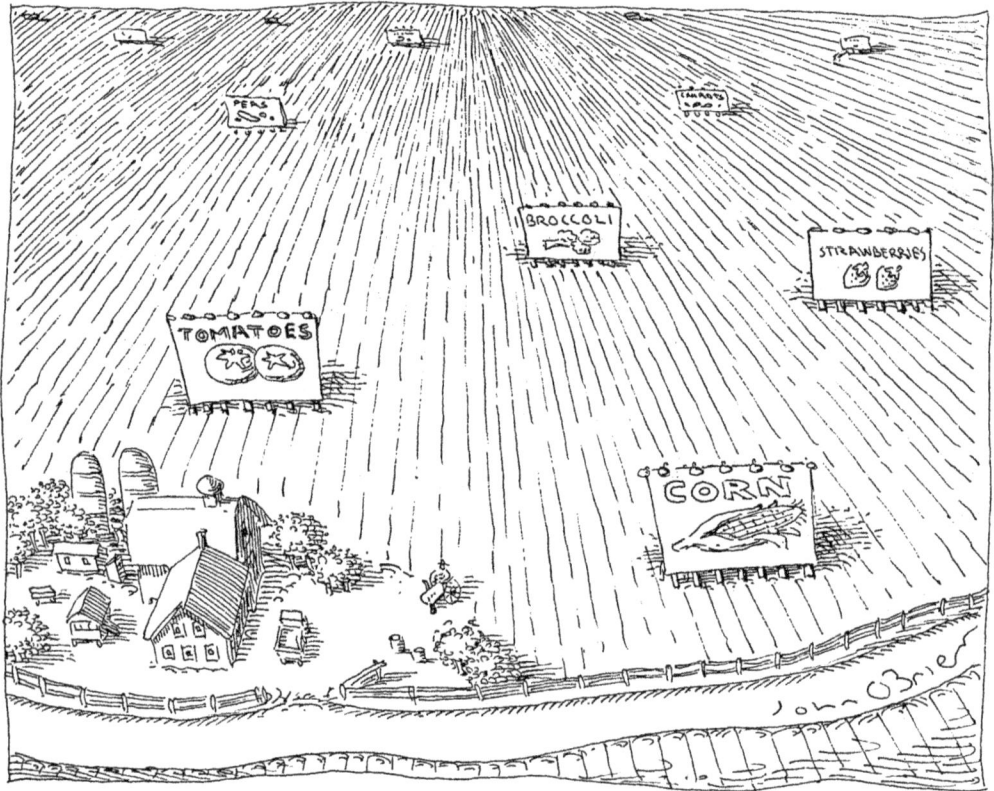

THE FLYING LAWN TIGERS

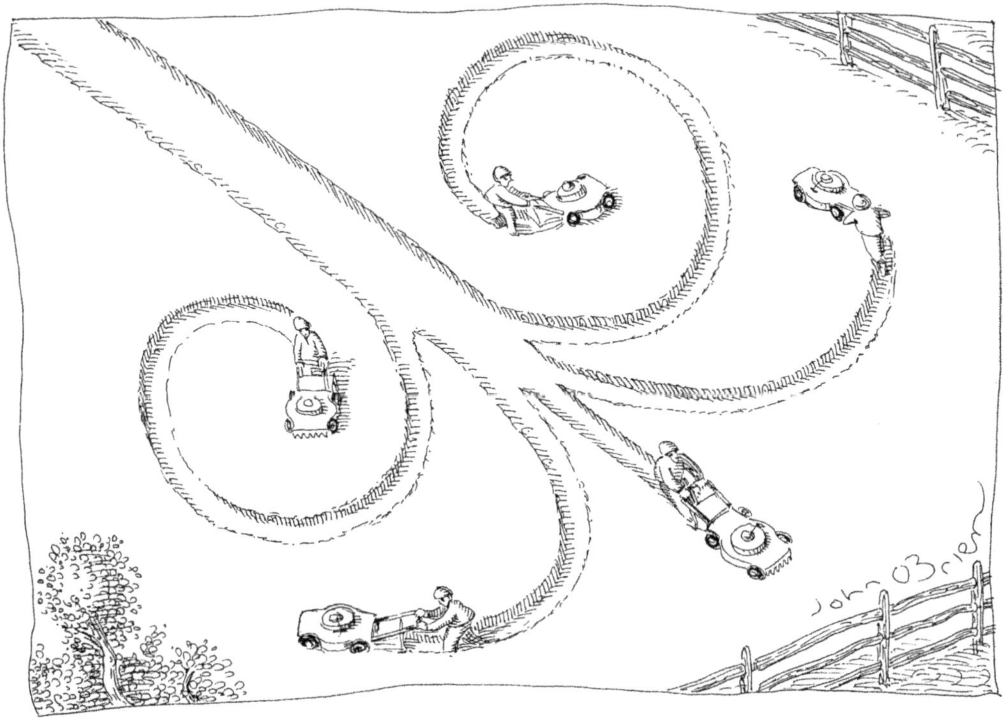
John O'Brien

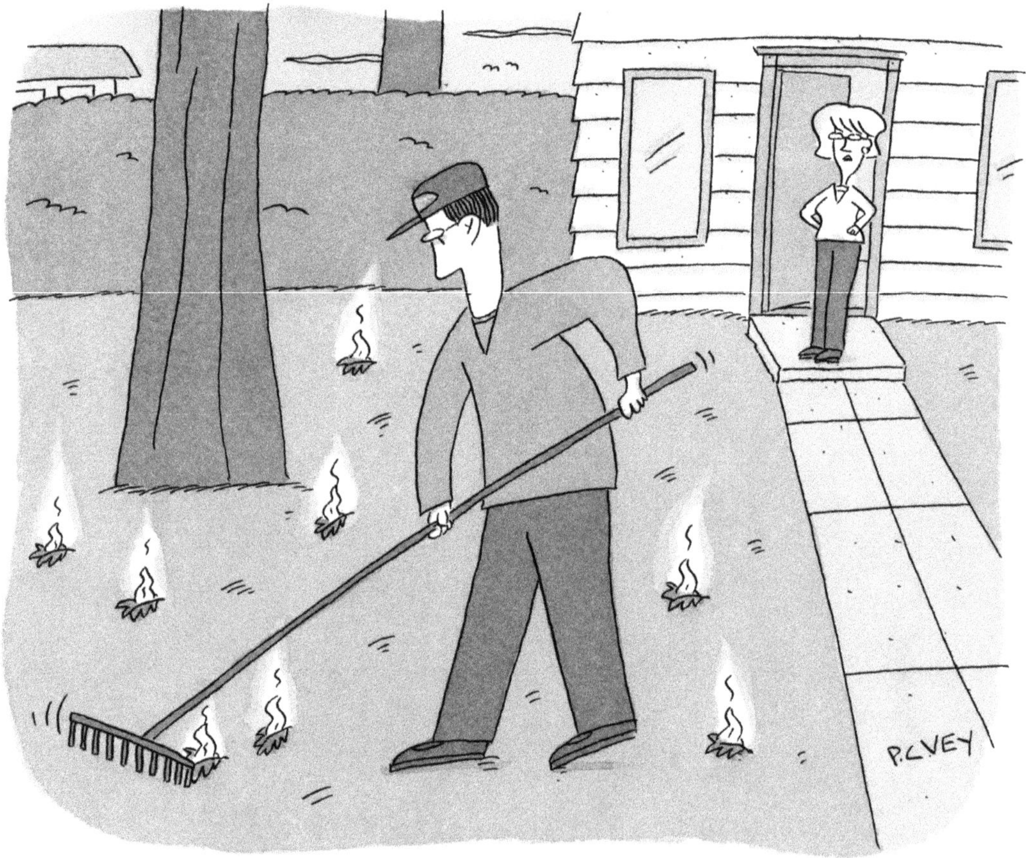
P.C.VEY

"Shouldn't you rake those up first and then set them on fire?"

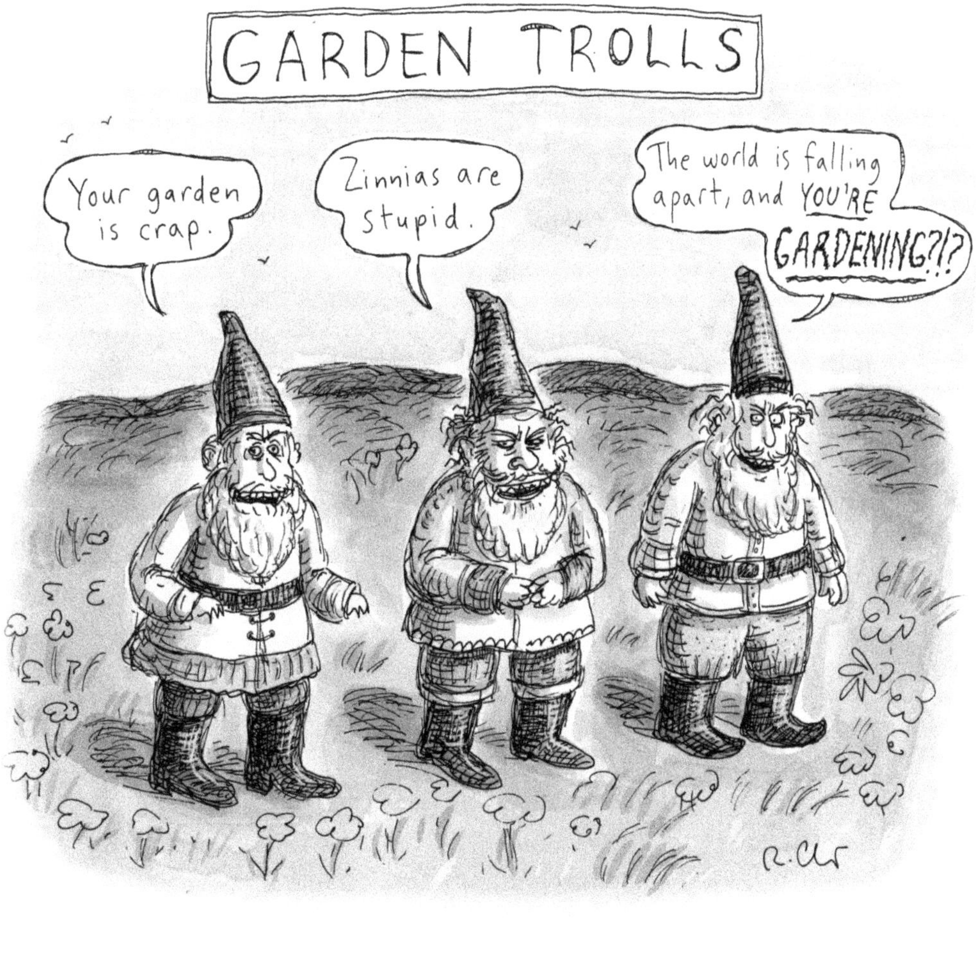
GARDEN TROLLS
Your garden is crap.
Zinnias are stupid.
The world is falling apart, and YOU'RE GARDENING?!?
R.Ch

Victoria Roberts

"The garden is my resume."

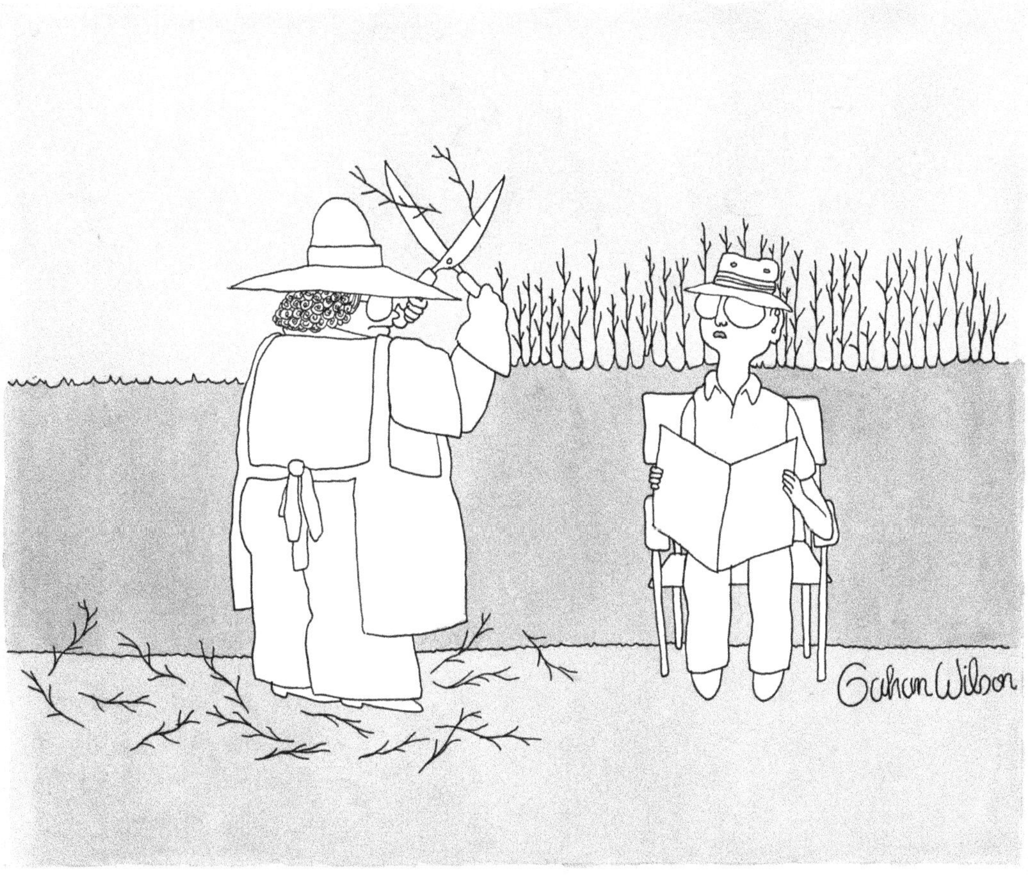
Gahan Wilson

"Hold it right there."

JUDI'S SEASONALS

ANNUALS   PERENNIALS   CENTENNIALS   MILLENNIALS

"I used to have a Green thumb but it was mainly for hedge funds."

"The hardest part was teaching him to use the hedge trimmers."

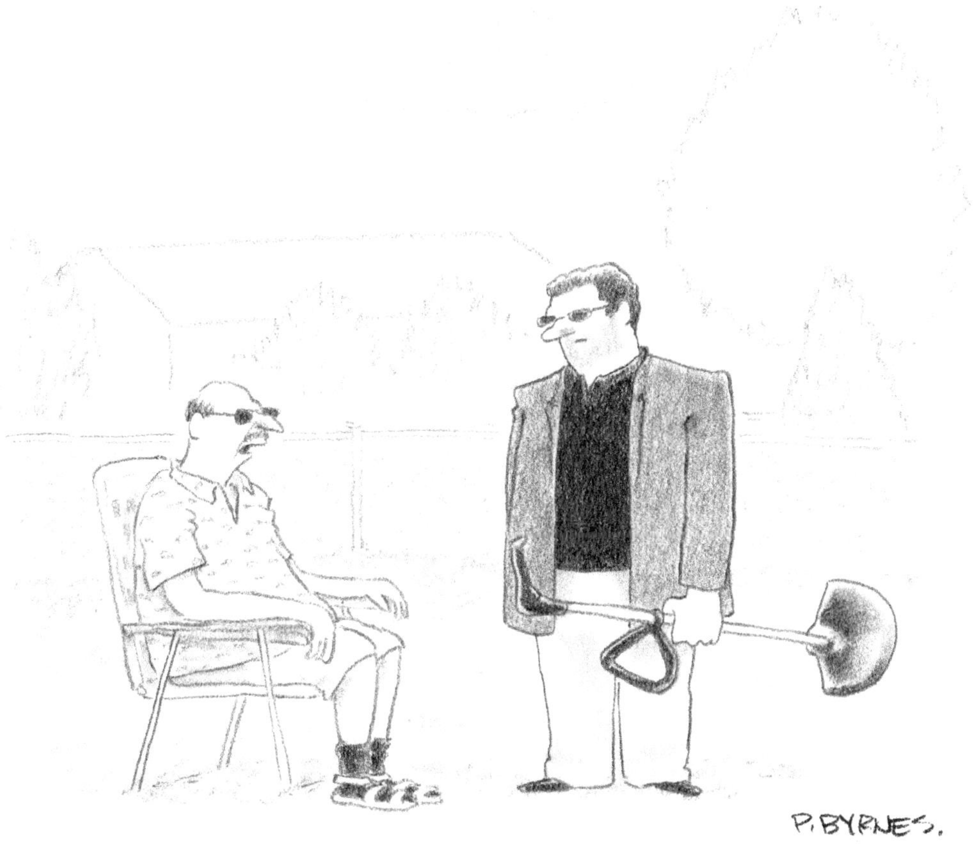
P. BYRNES.

"The weeds—I want 'em whacked."

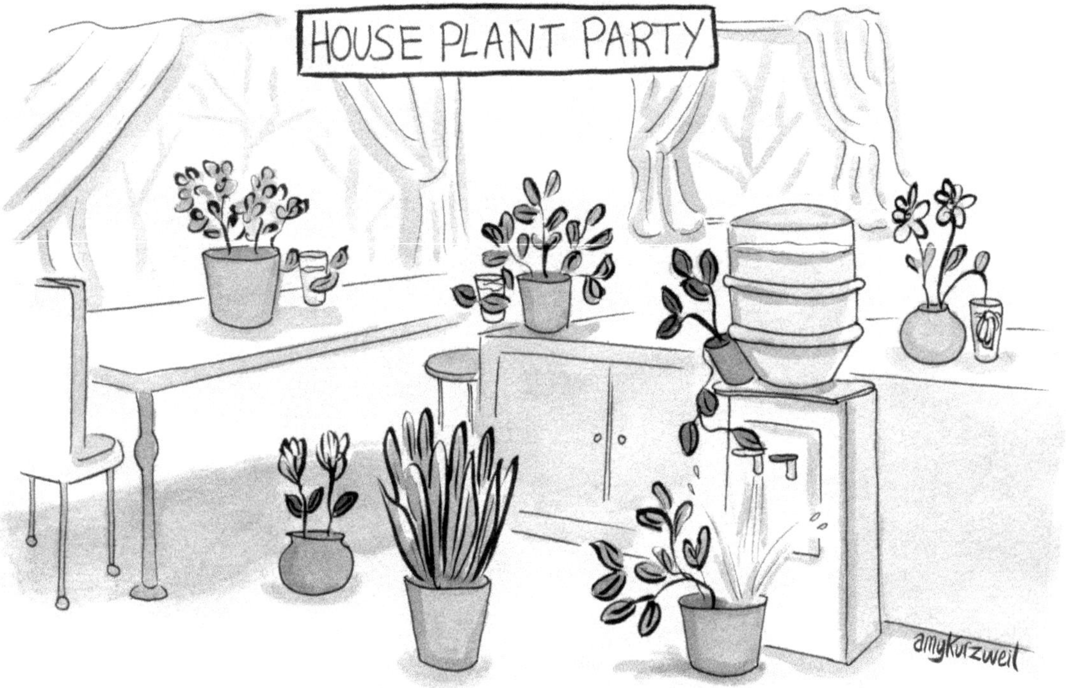
HOUSE PLANT PARTY
amyKurzweil

"Chug! Chug! Chug!"

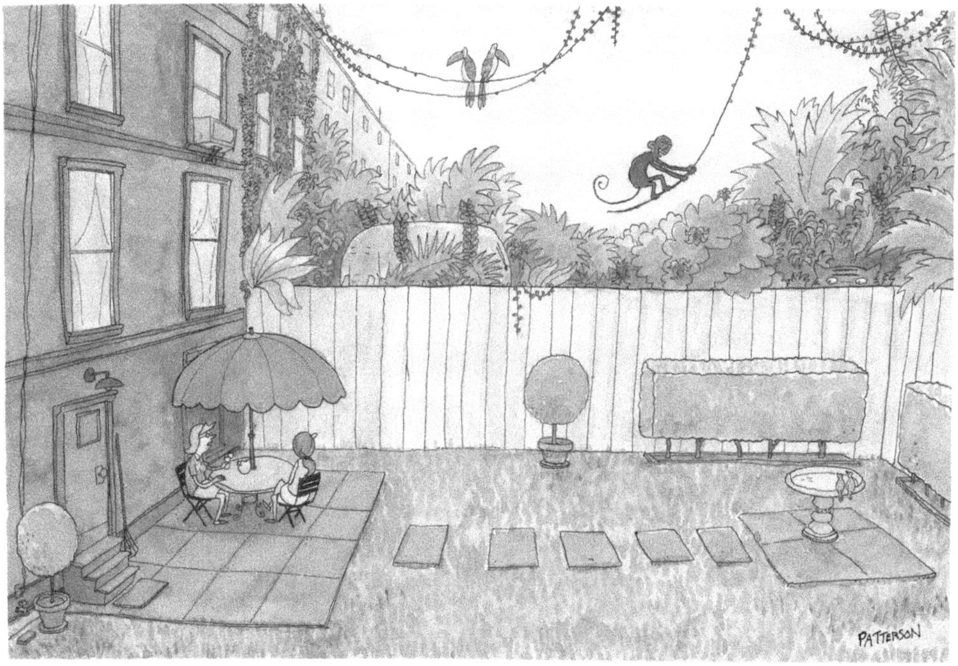
PATTERSON

"Boy, they really let their yard go."

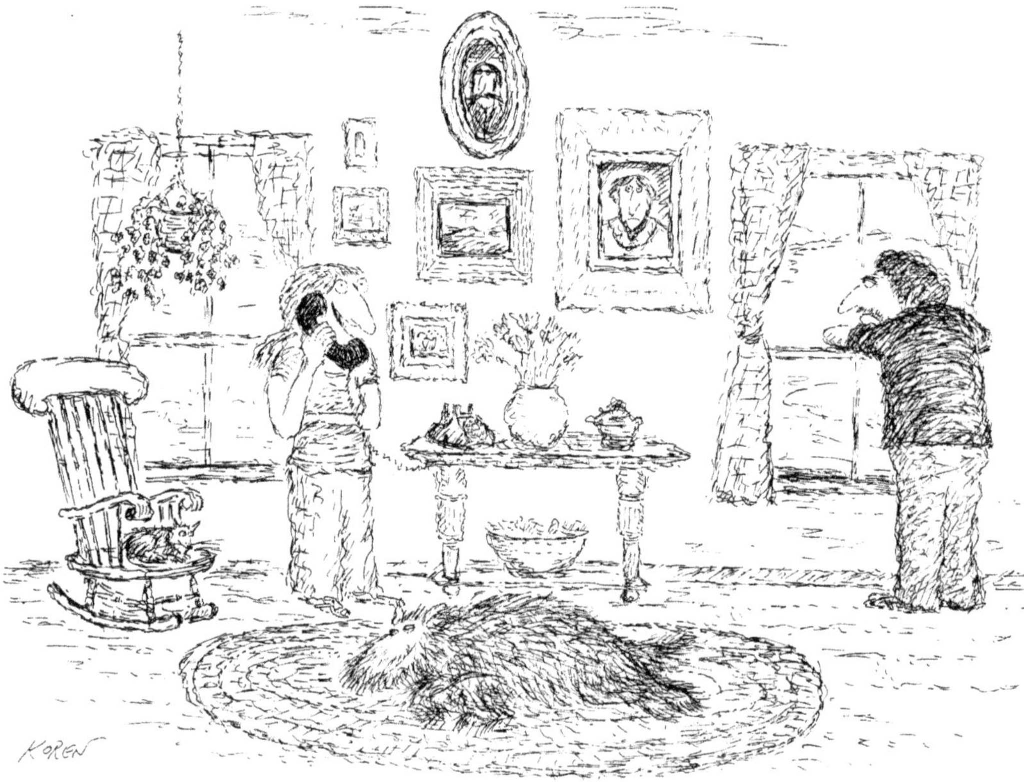
KOREN

"Everything's just fine. The garden is coming in beautifully, and Jeremy is in his usual rage."

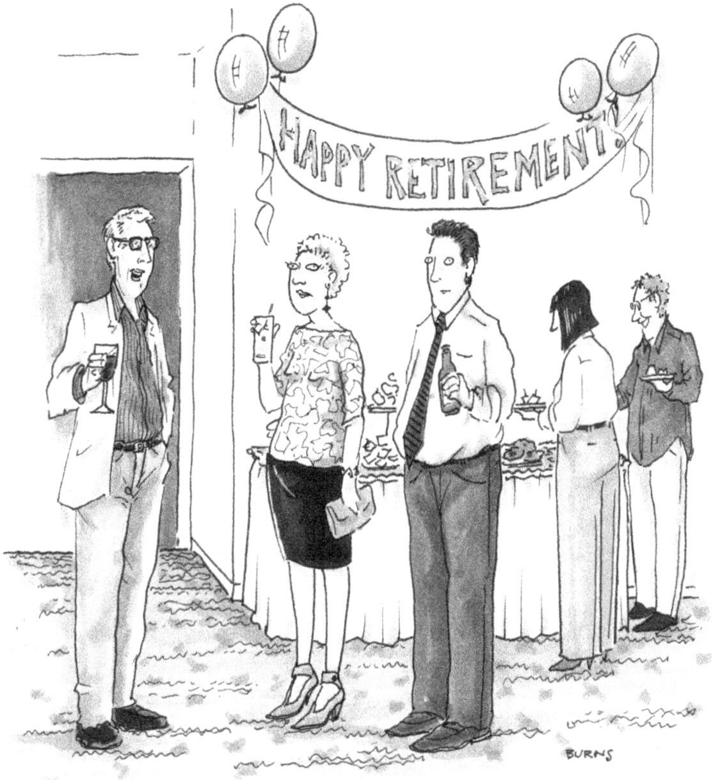
HAPPY RETIREMENT!
BURNS

"No plans set in stone yet, but I'll probably spend some time getting on my wife's last nerve, maybe hyperfocus on the lawn."

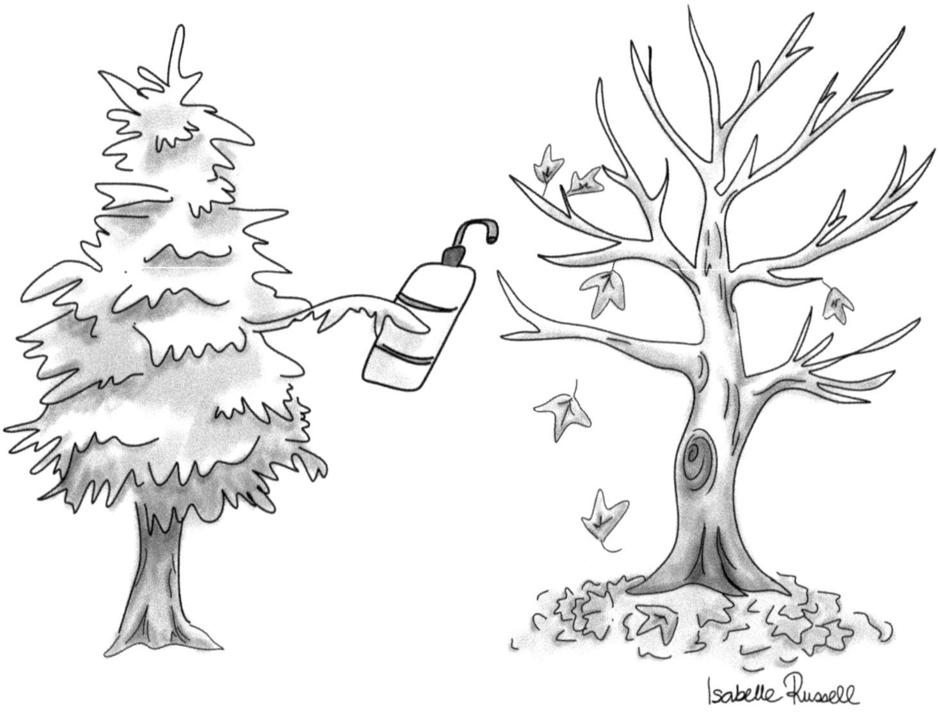
Isabelle Russell

"Here, try this anti-dandruff fertiliser my gardener recommended."

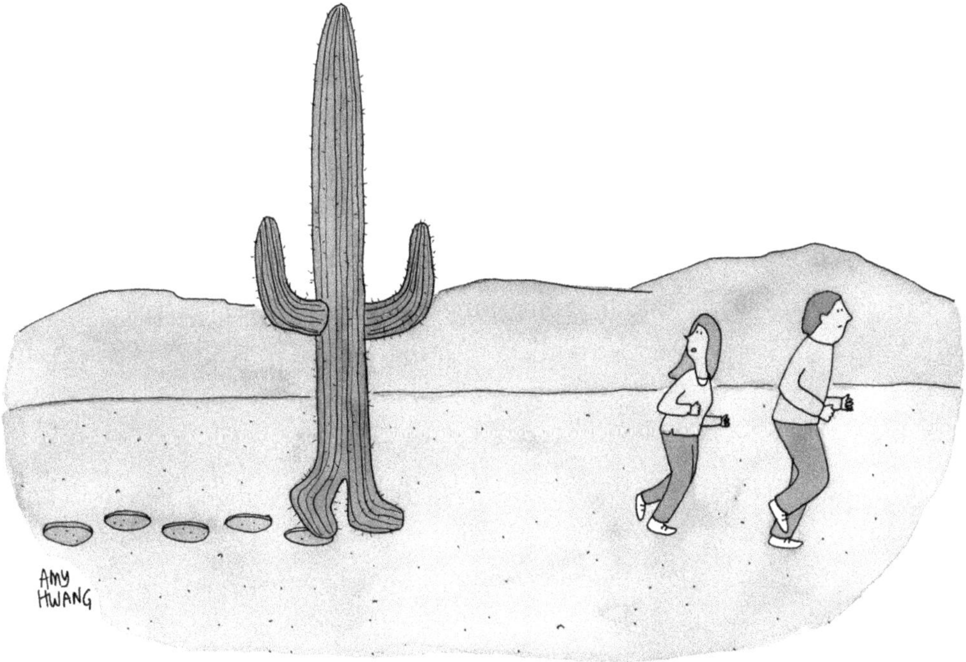
AMY
HWANG

"I thought you said it wouldn't need much attention."

ANNUALS
$6.00

PERENNIALS
$10.00

ETERNALS
$749.95

S. HARRIS

"Here's to us, kid—and the healing powers of raw juices."

GOING FULL TERRARIUM

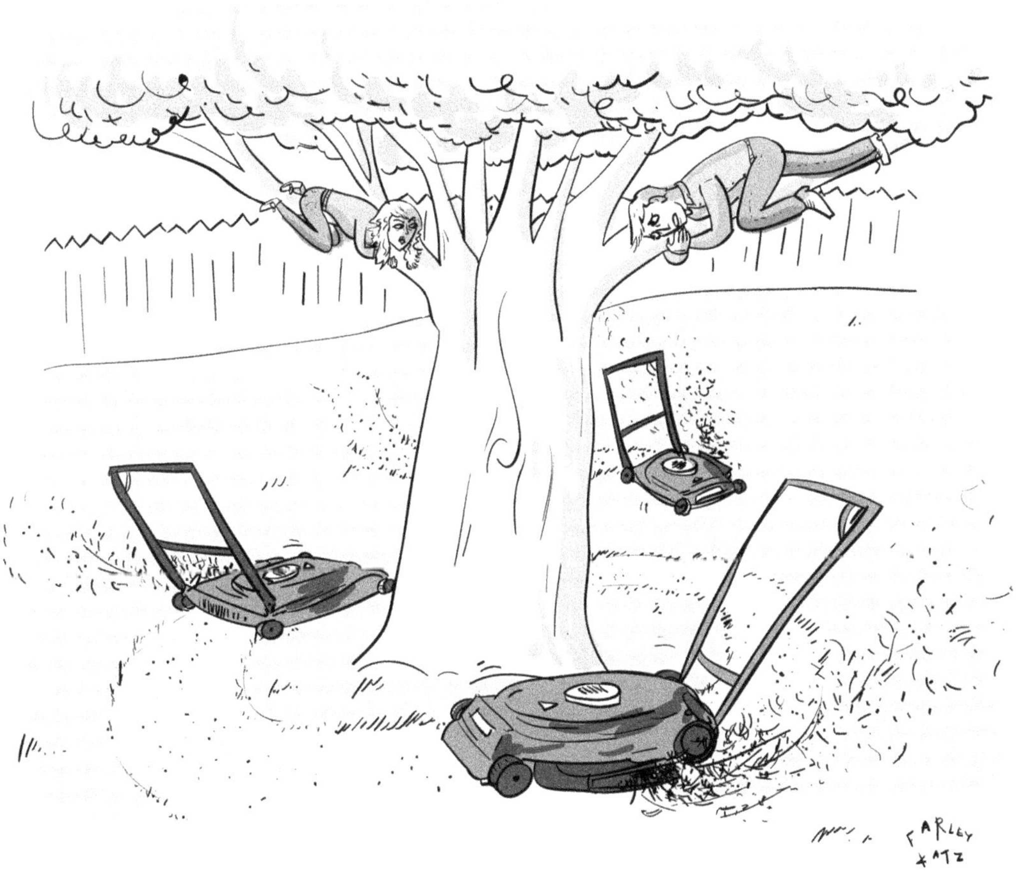
FARLEY KATZ

"Autonomous lawnmowers were a bad idea. I see that now."

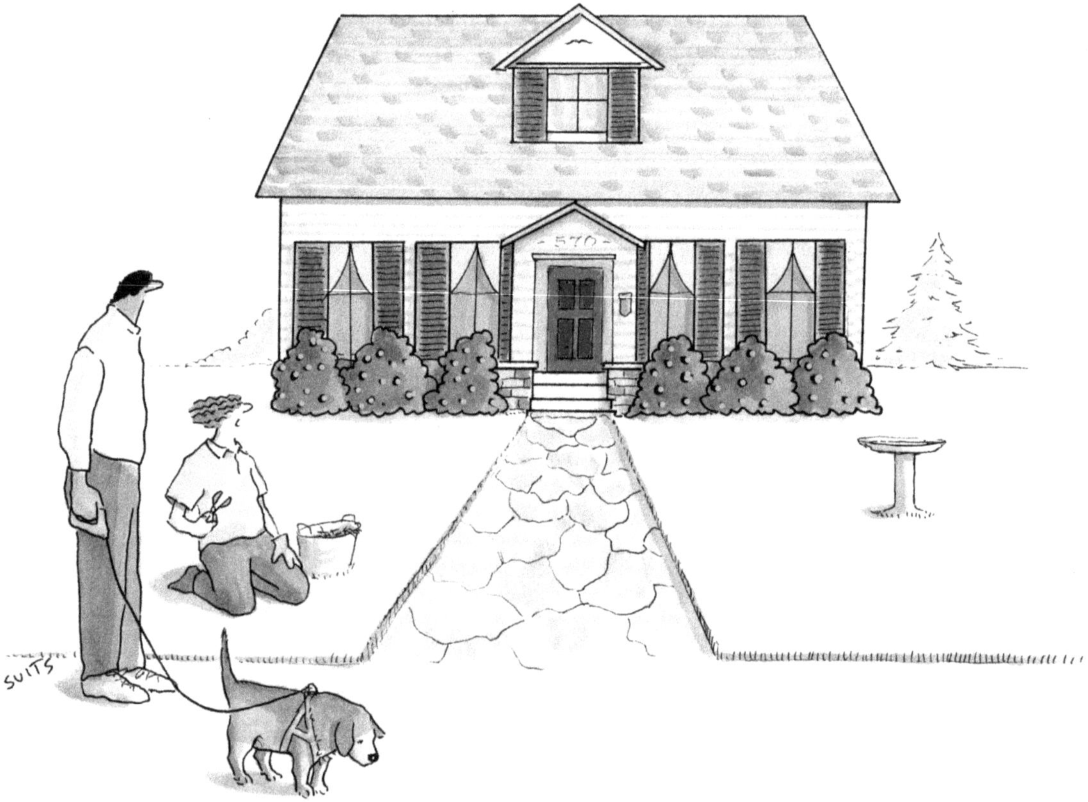
570
SUITS

"Don't be fooled. Chaos reigns."

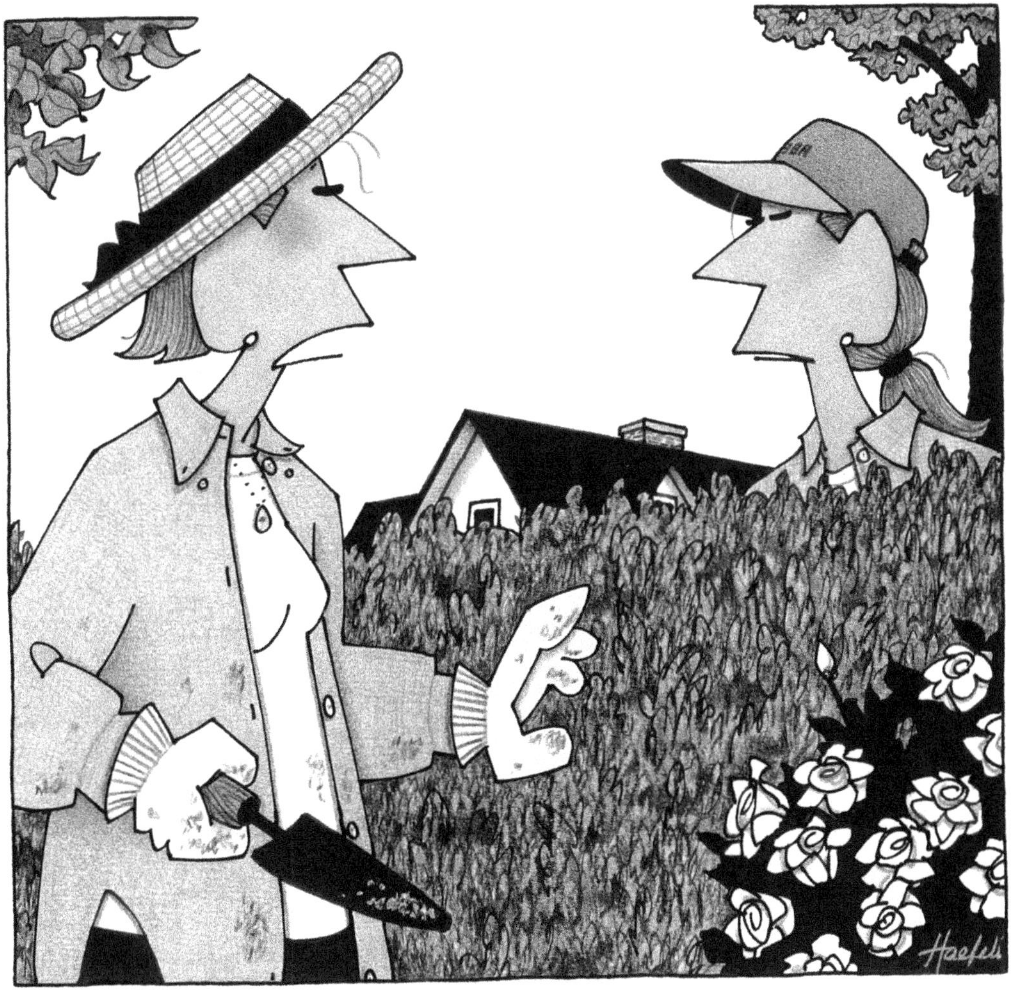
Haefeli

*"We're thinking of moving to another part of the country—
somewhere between Lyme disease and killer bees."*

JUNK DRAWER

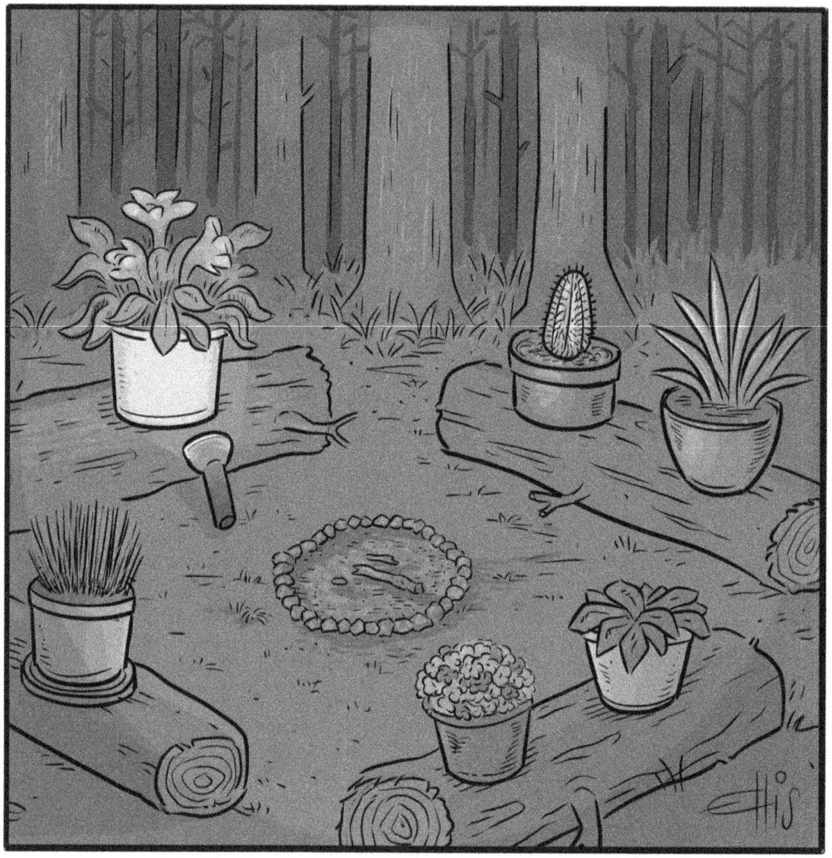

"And that's when they left for vacation!"

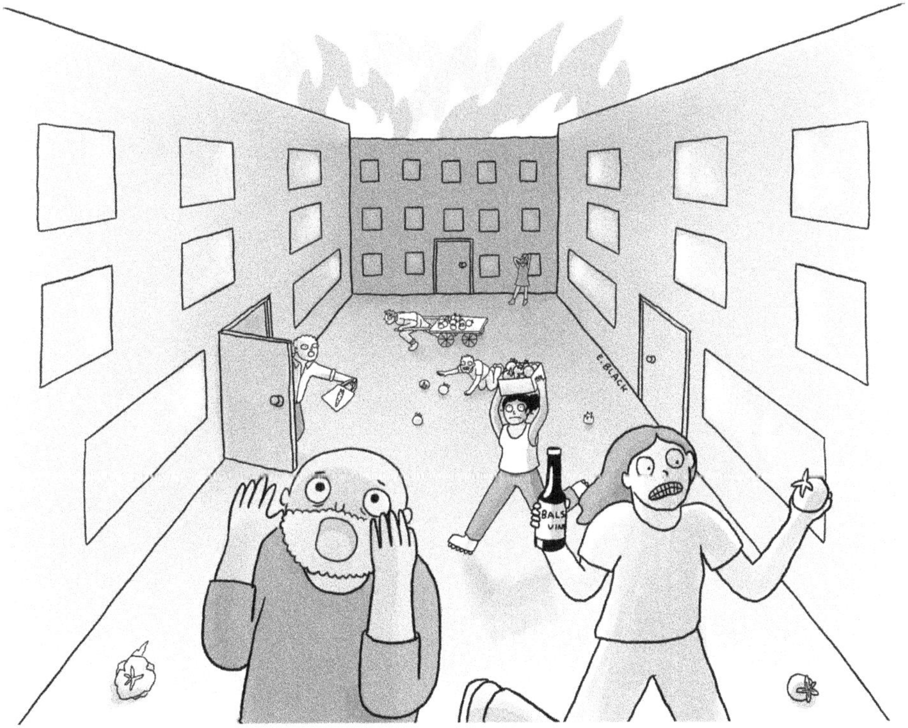
E. BLACK

"Quick! It's the 45 minutes a year when tomatoes taste incredible!"

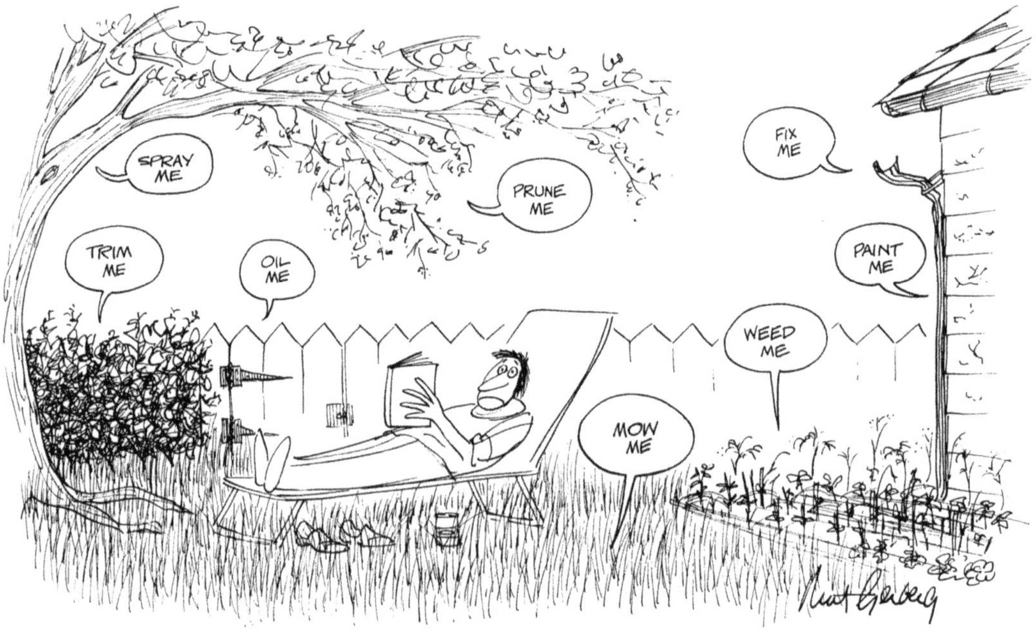
SPRAY ME
PRUNE ME
FIX ME
TRIM ME
OIL ME
PAINT ME
WEED ME
MOW ME

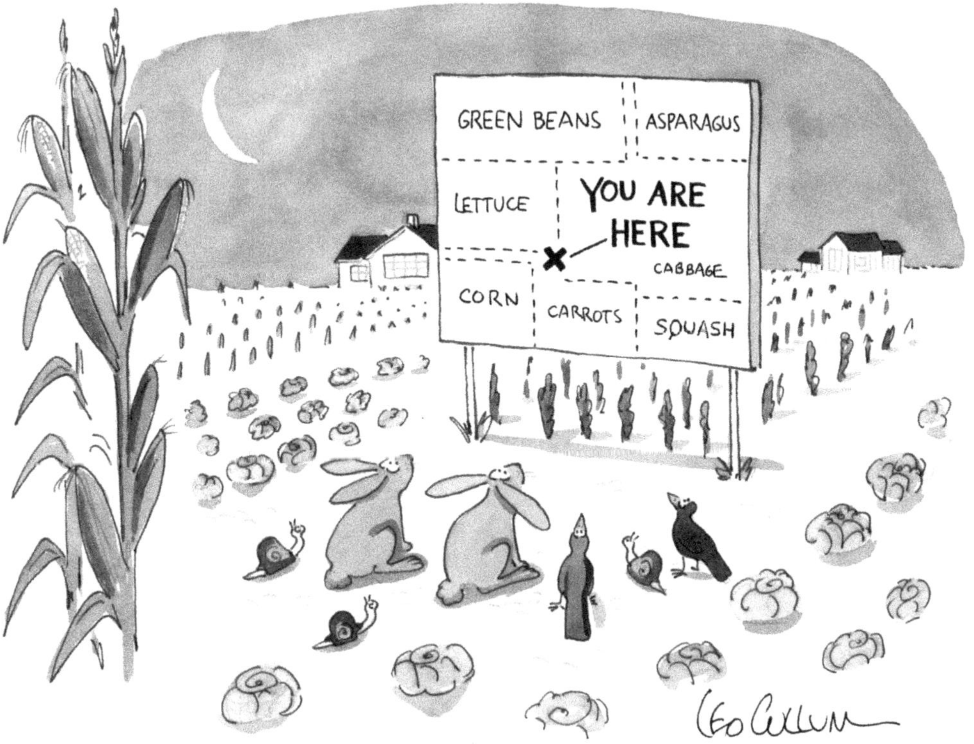
GREEN BEANS
ASPARAGUS
LETTUCE
YOU ARE HERE
CABBAGE
CORN
CARROTS
SQUASH
LEO CULLUM

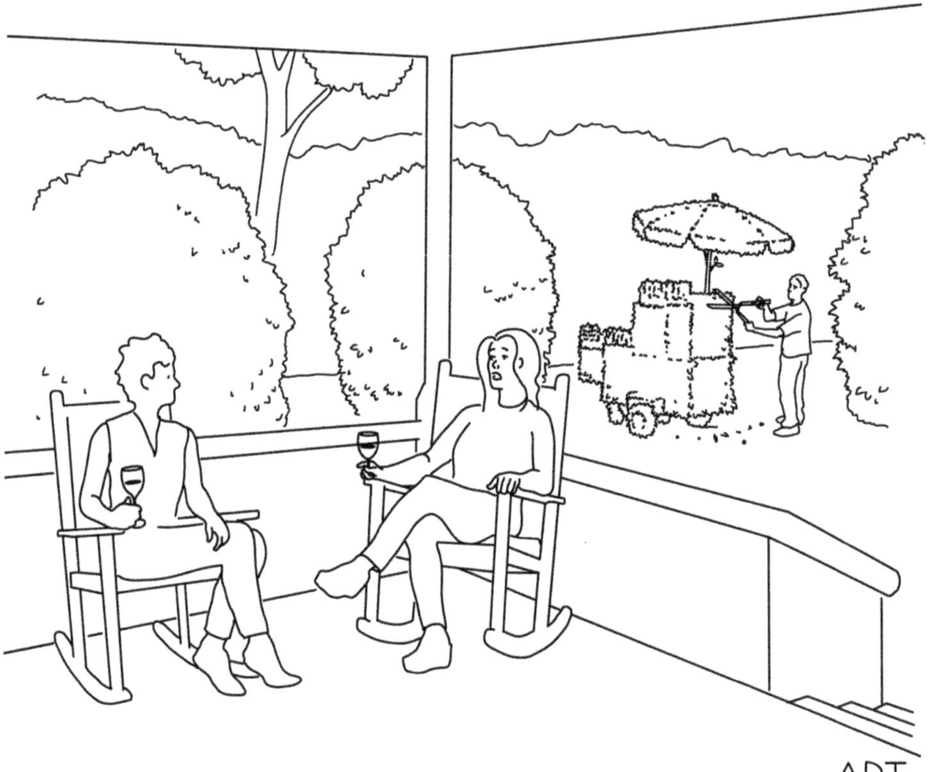
ADT

"It's great having all the space,
but Dan has been missing the city a bit."

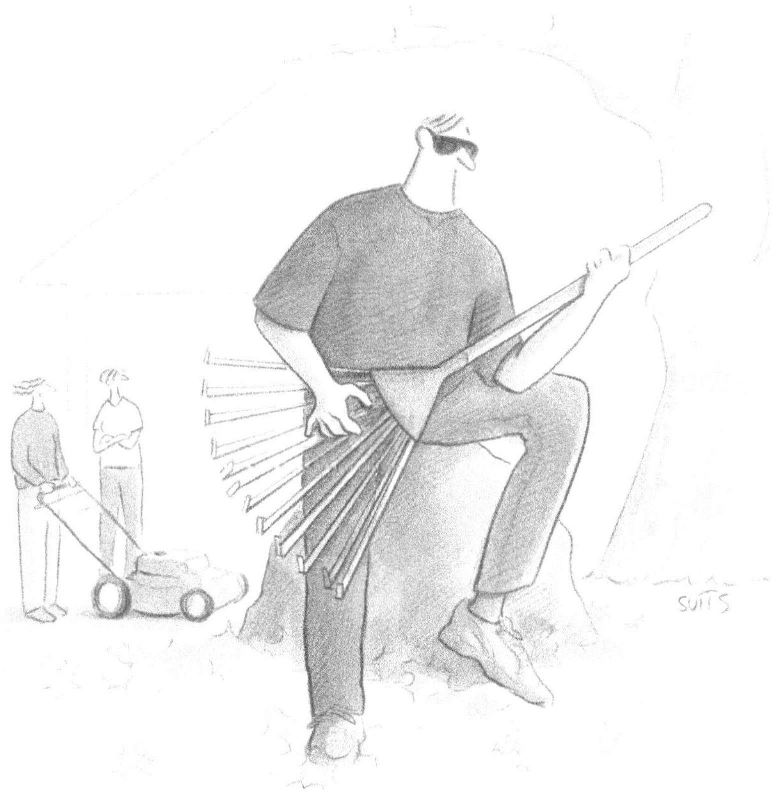
SUITS

"Fall makes him sad."

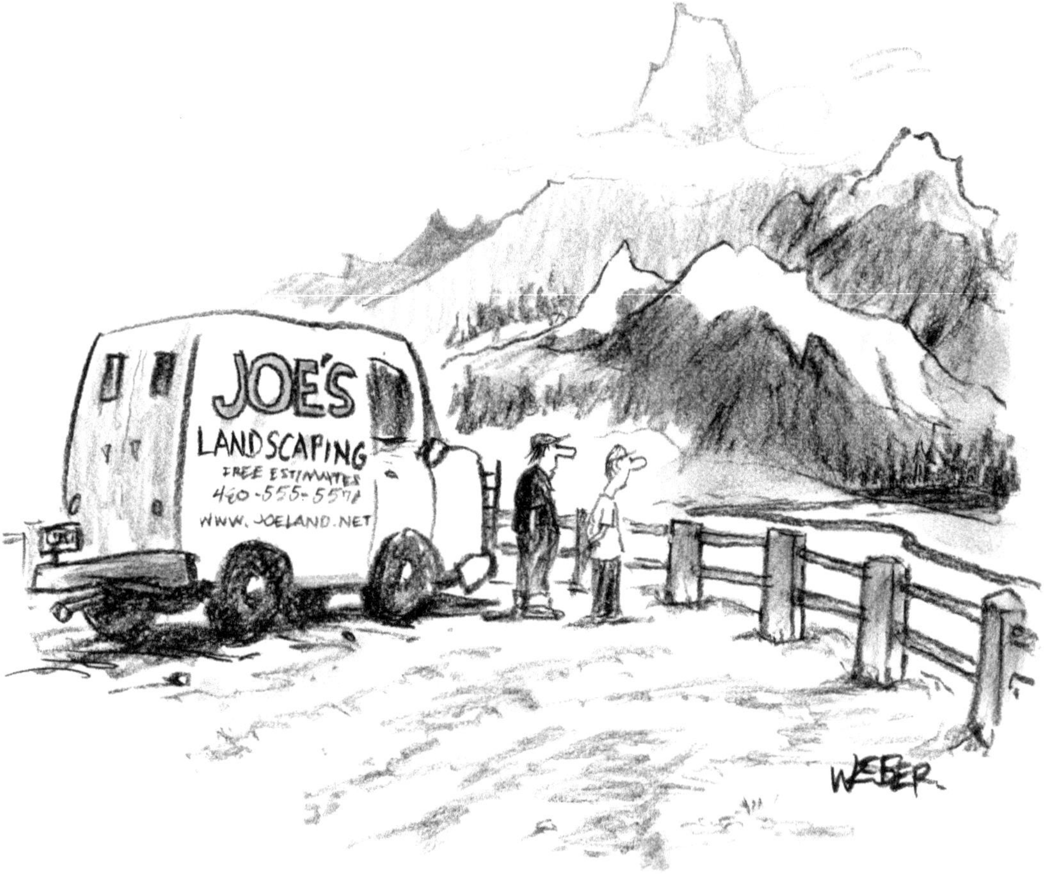
JOE'S
LANDSCAPING
FREE ESTIMATES
WWW. JOELAND.NET
WEBER

"I would have done this differently."

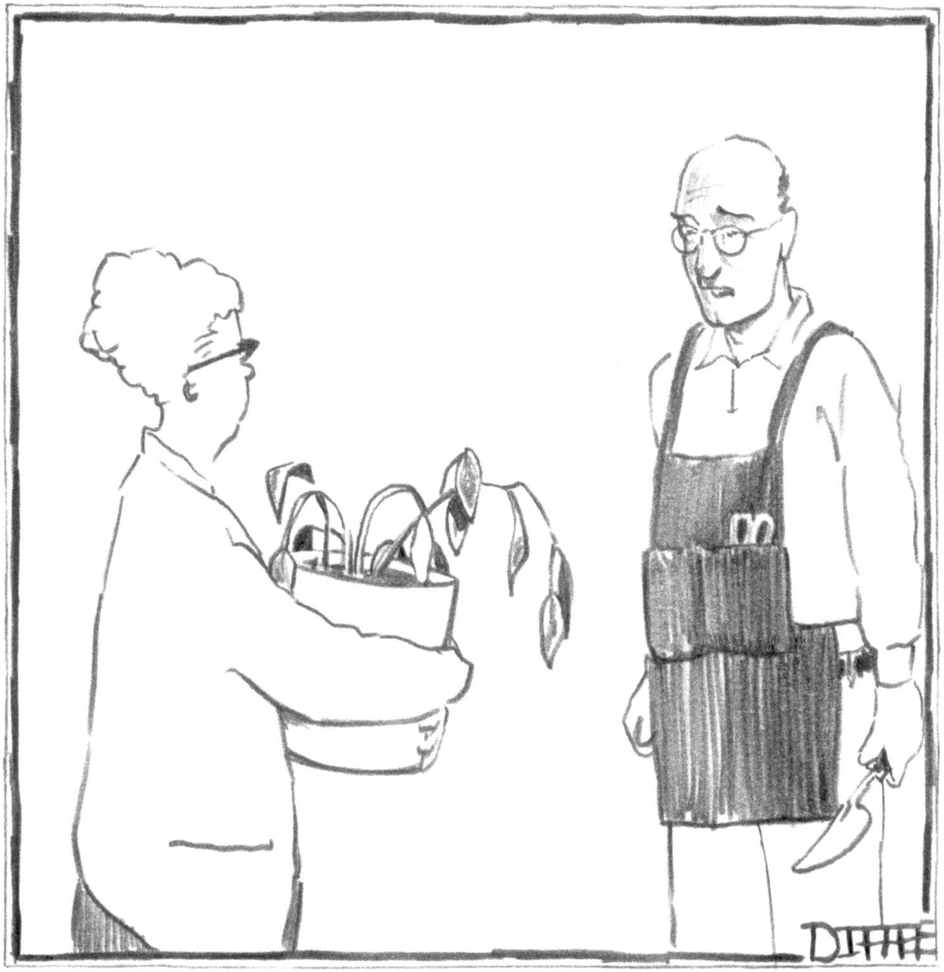
DIFFEE

"It needs more sun and less gangster rap."

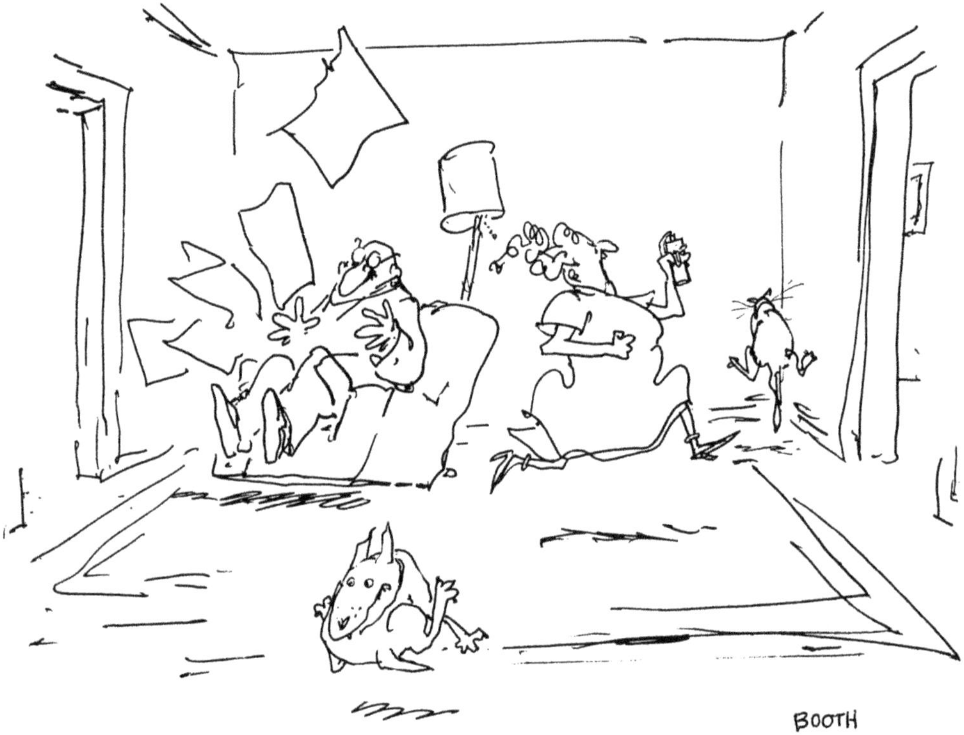
BOOTH

"Aphids on the heliotrope!"

"After spending all day out there I'm so calmed by a limited color palette and some simple, clean lines."

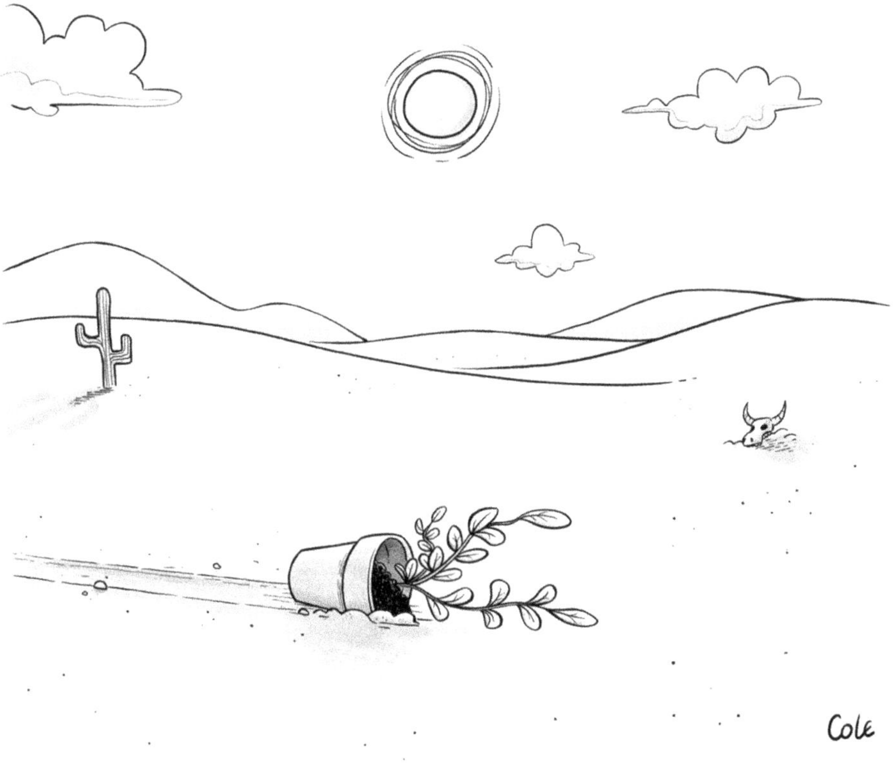
Cole

"Water... water... but not too much."

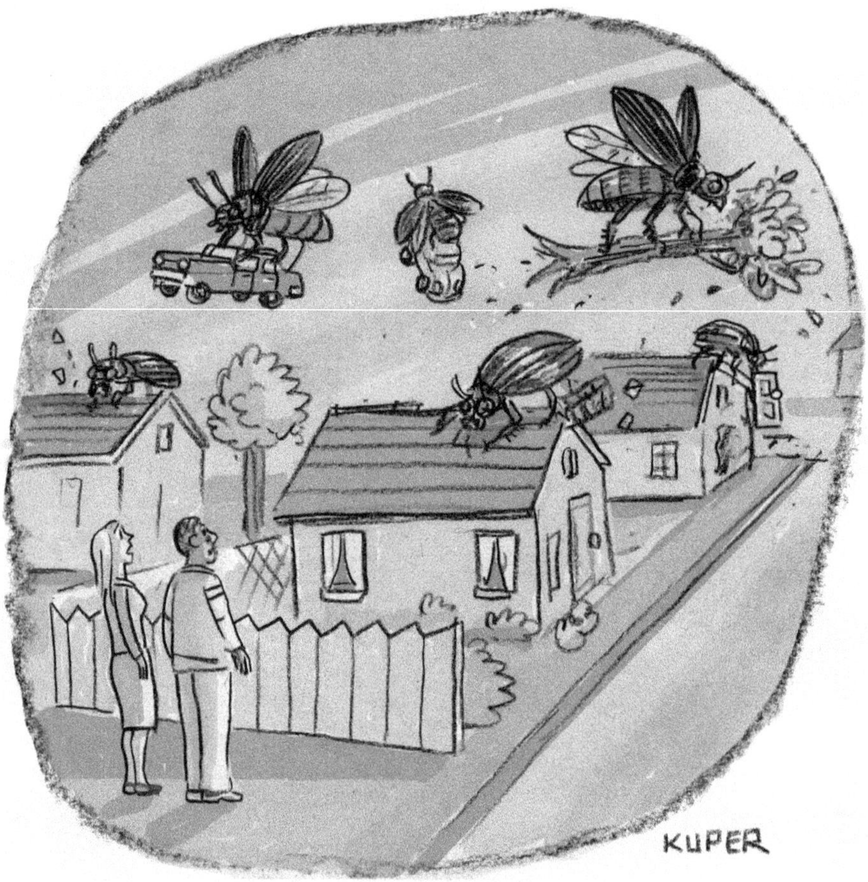
KUPER

"Thank goodness they're only seasonal."

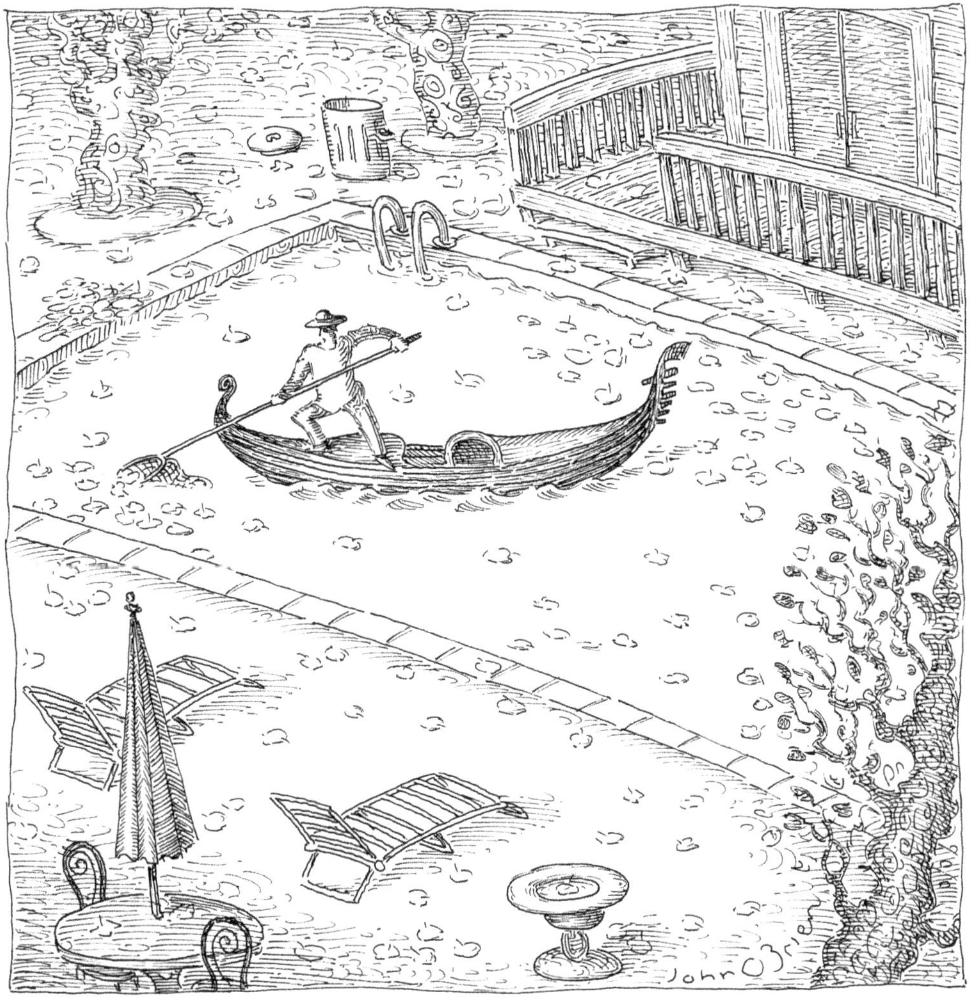
John O'Brien

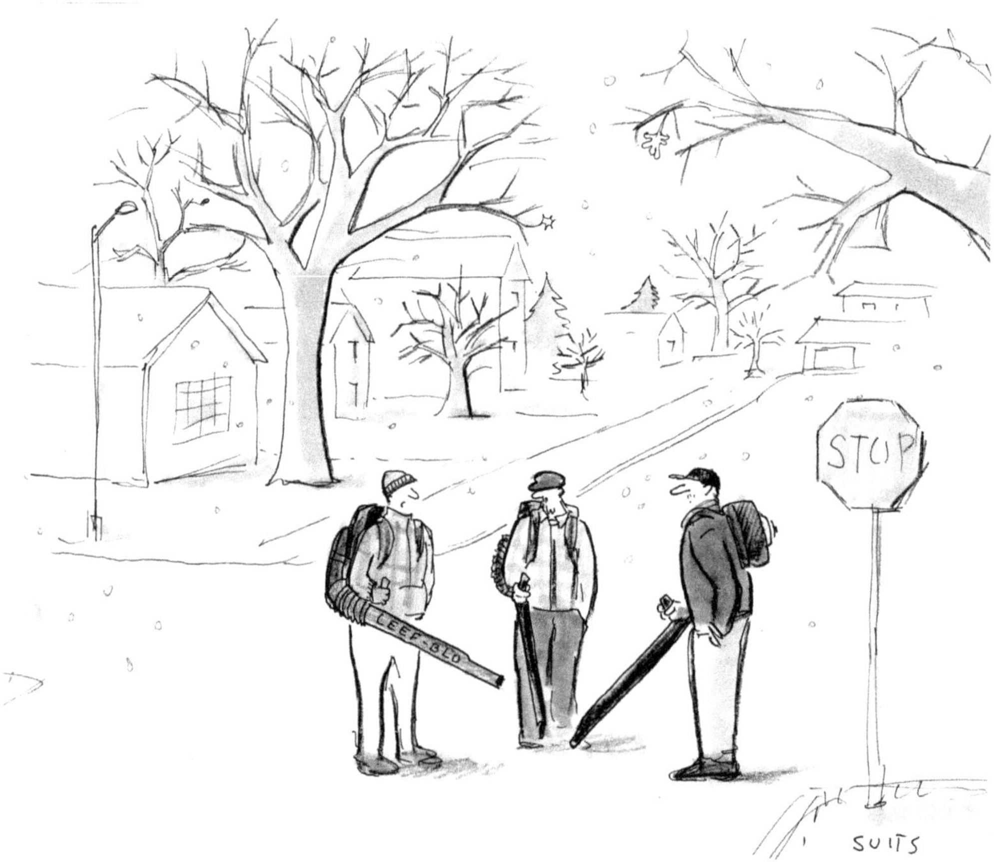
LEEF-BLO
STOP
SUITS

"We could start a band."

GARDEN SUPPLIES

SPECIAL!

NOW!
IN YOUR
OWN GARDEN!
GROW THE
FLOWERS
FEATURED IN
RECORD-BREAKING
WORKS OF ART!!

IRIS SUNFLOWER

W Miller

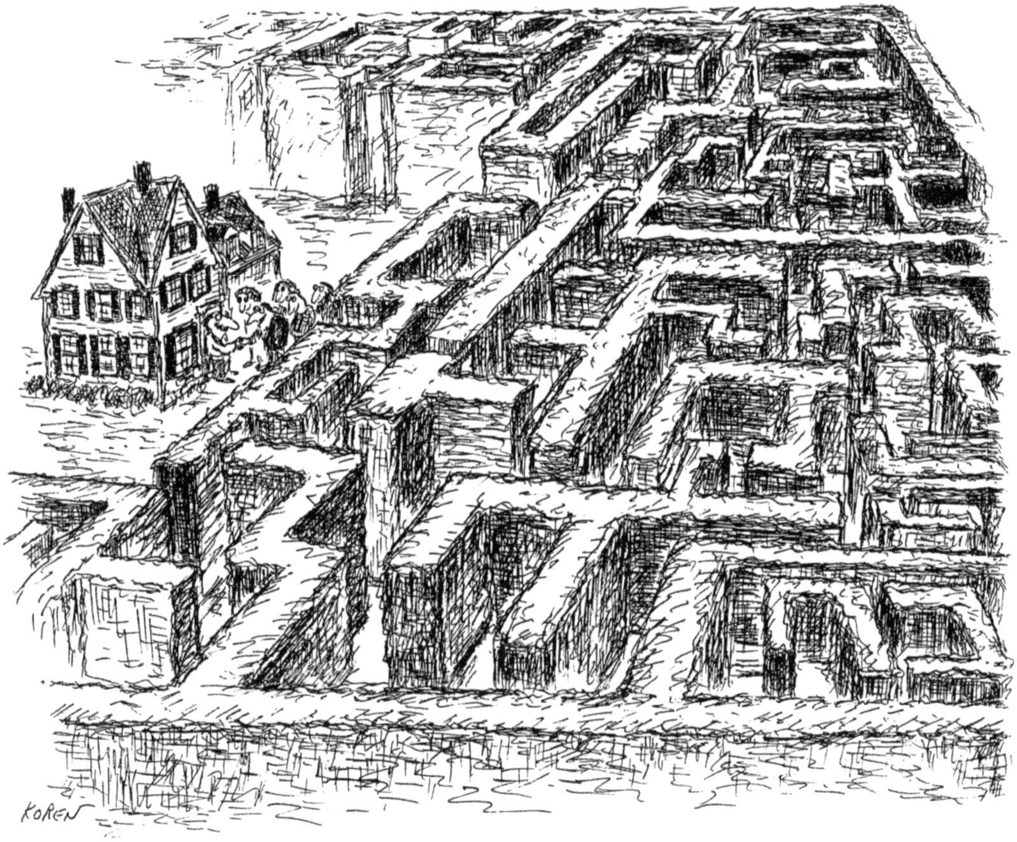
KOREN

"Your instructions were perfect."

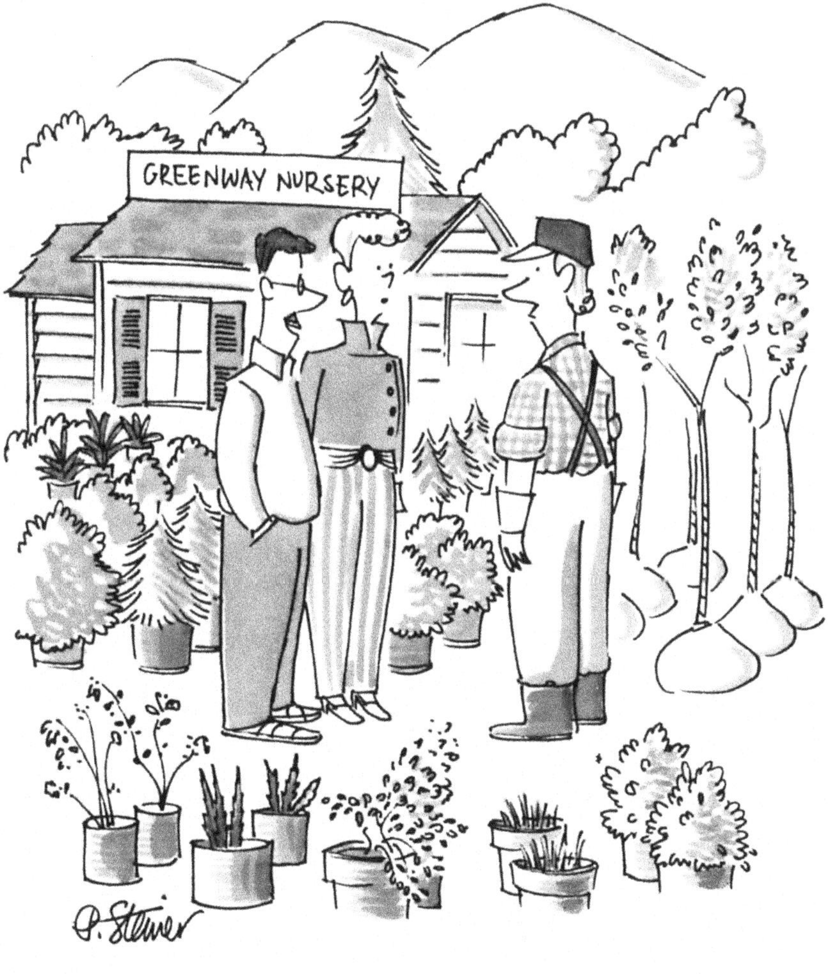
GREENWAY NURSERY
P. Steiner

"I think we're ready for a tree."

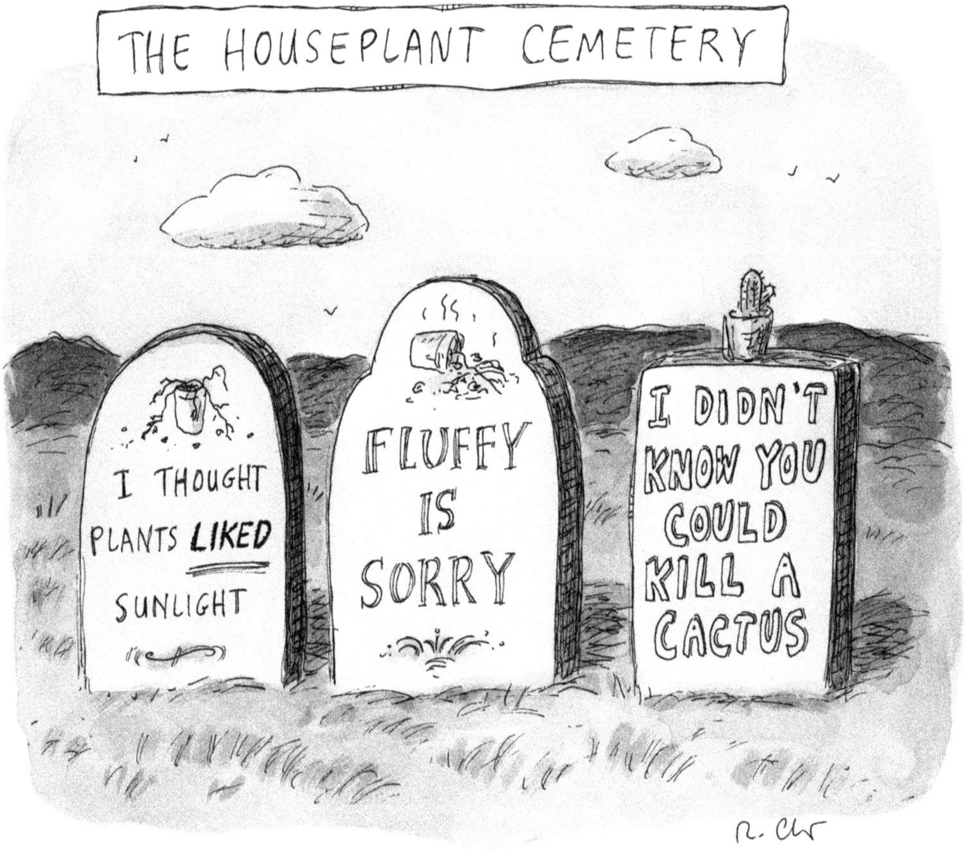
THE HOUSEPLANT CEMETERY
I THOUGHT PLANTS LIKED SUNLIGHT
FLUFFY IS SORRY
I DIDN'T KNOW YOU COULD KILL A CACTUS
R. Chr

"They're all pretty, but this one is my favorite."

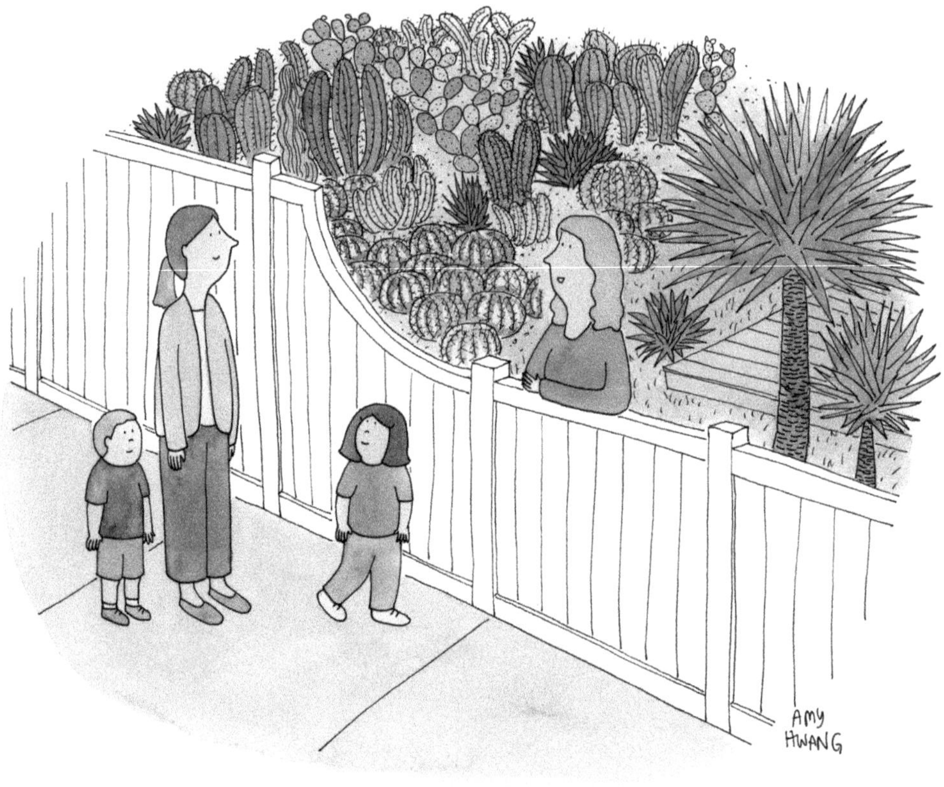
AMY
HWANG

"Your munchkins are always welcome to play in my garden."

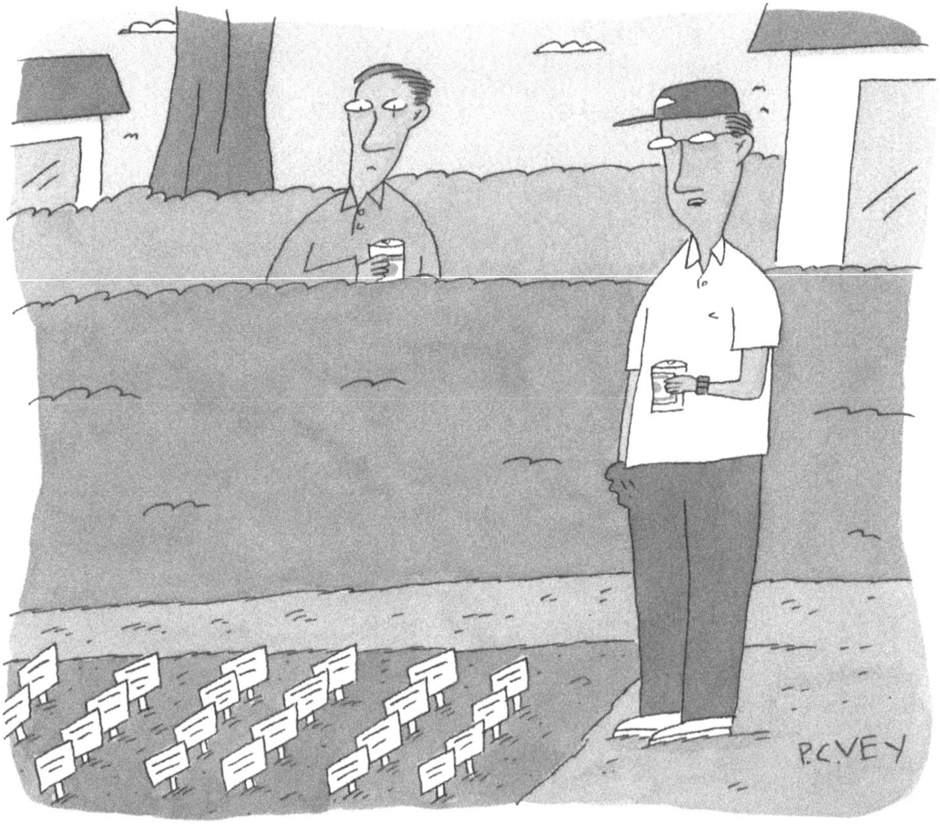
P.C.VEY

"This year I'm just planting the little signs."

HAPPY HOUR
AT THE
STAMEN & PISTIL

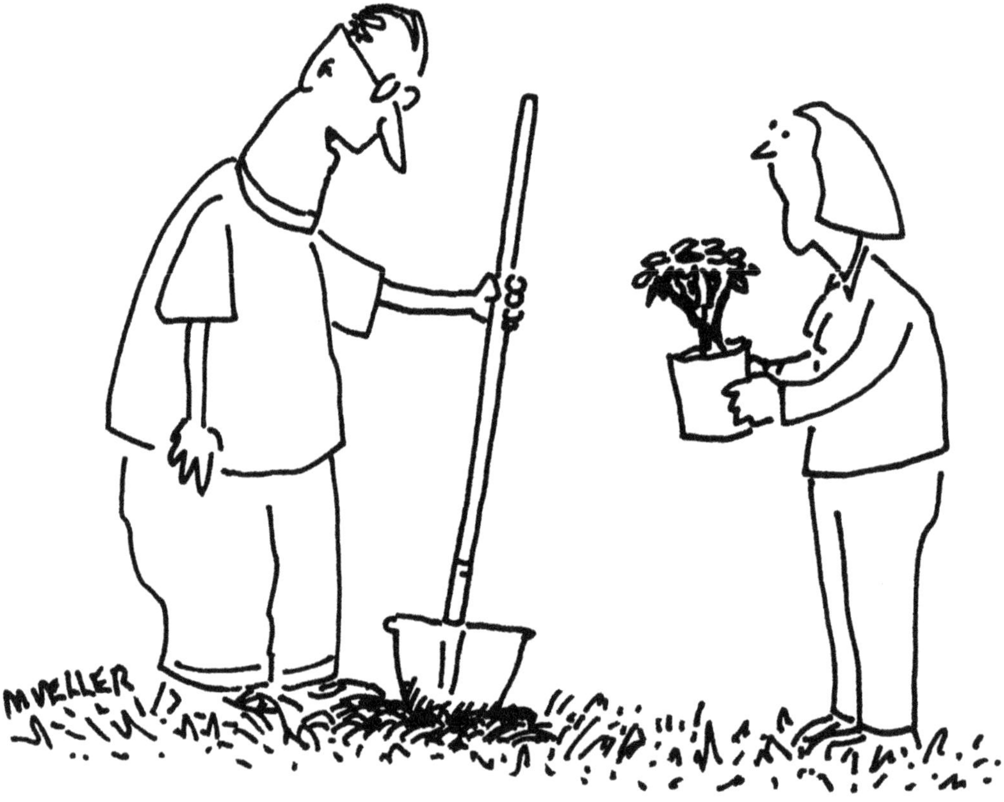
MUELLER 17

"Well, I'll be darned. There's a really nice hardwood floor under here."

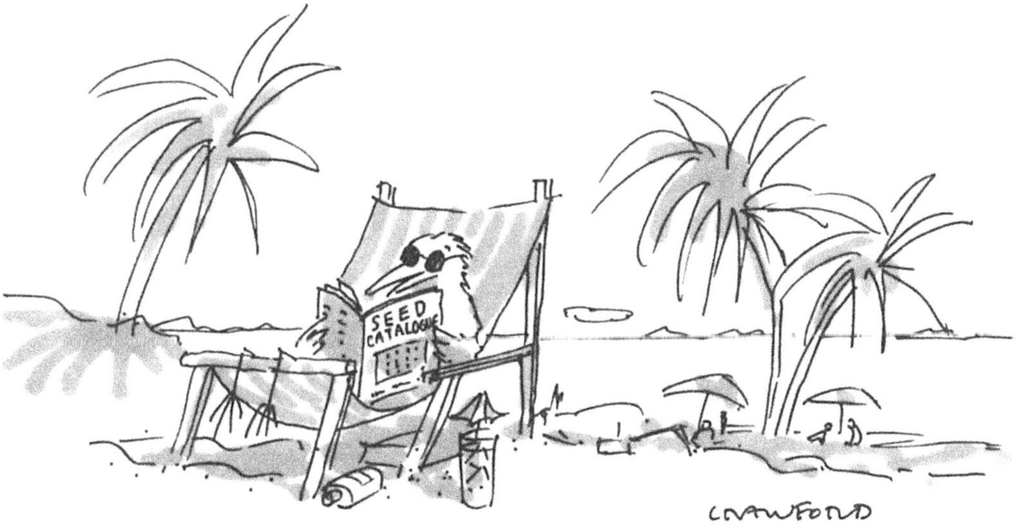
SEED CATALOGUE
CRAWFORD

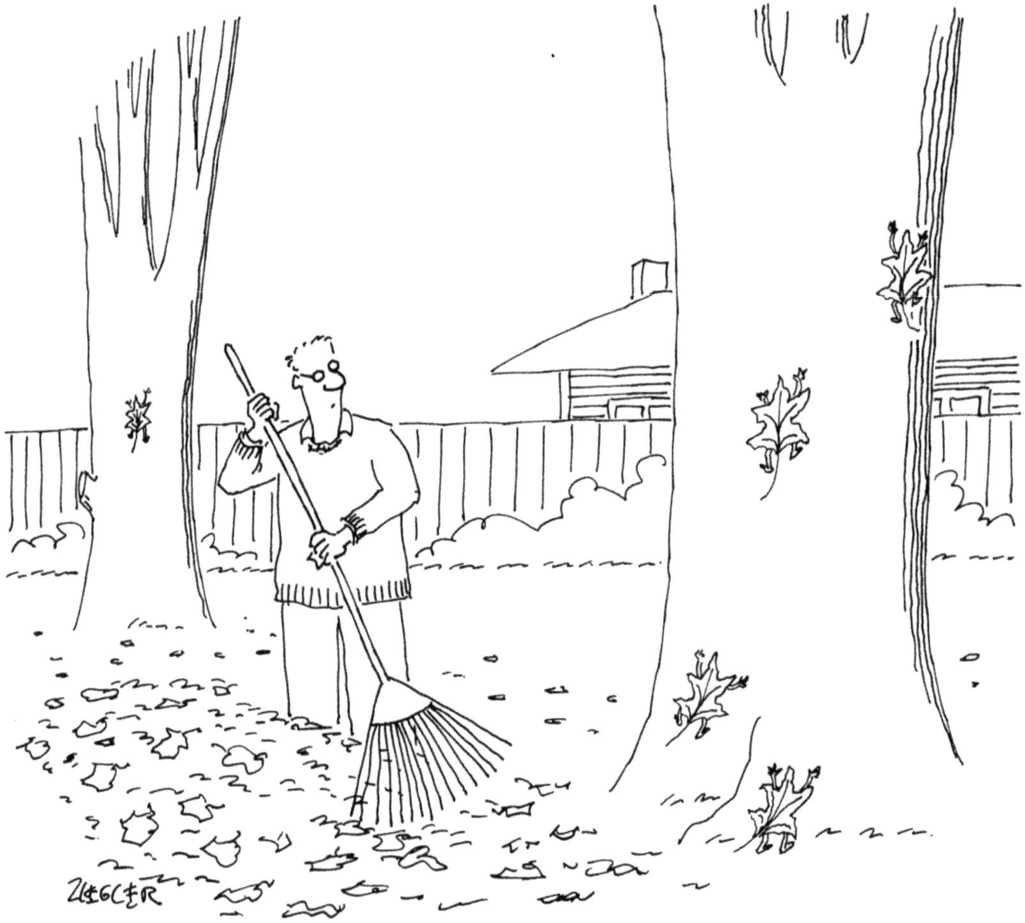
ZIEGLER

"I can say with certainty that we can
all look forward to a great summer season."

"My therapist suggested I redirect my anger into
landscaping and gardening!"

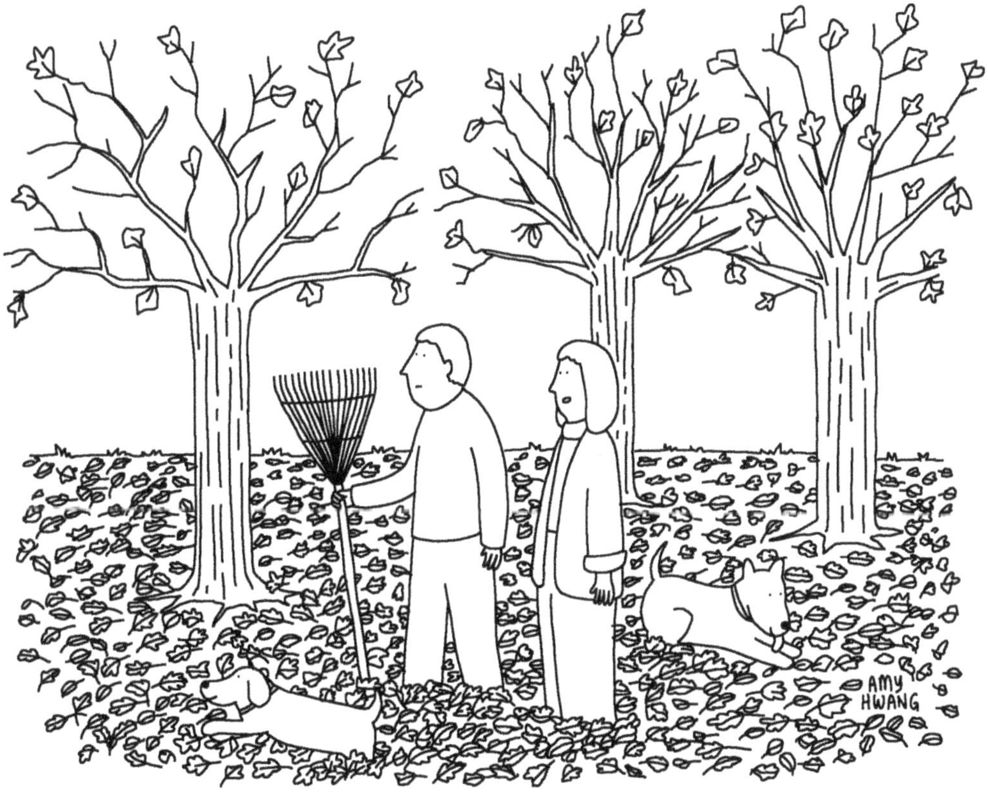
AMY
HWANG

"Next time, don't rake with the dogs."

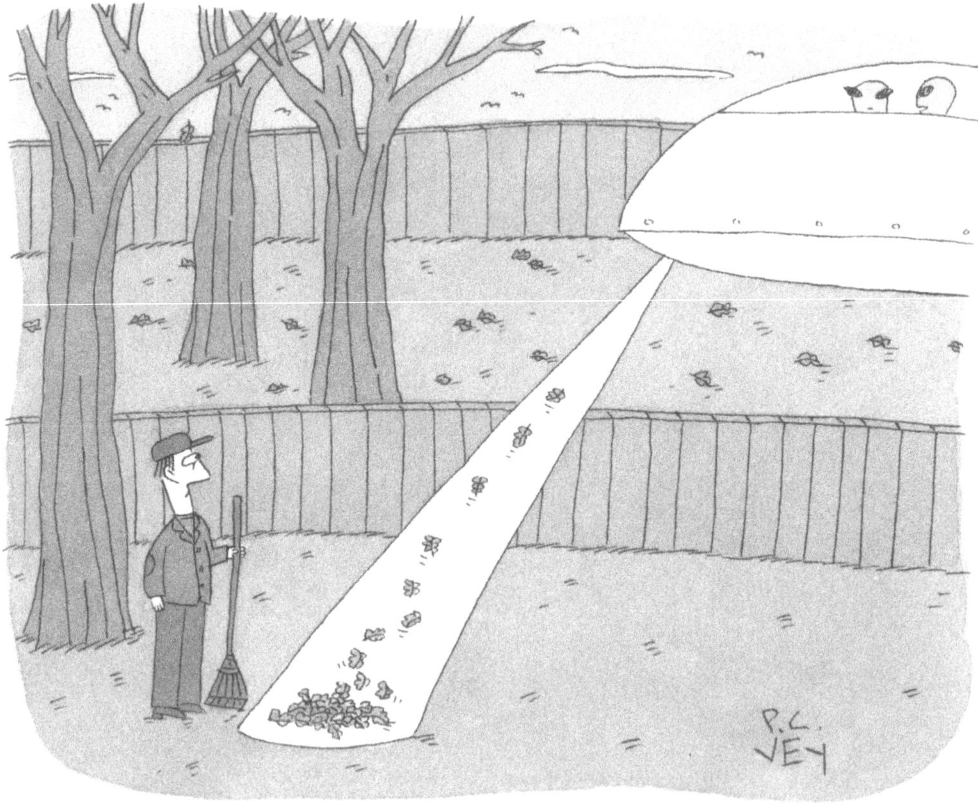
P.C. VEY

"Can't wait to see the look on his face when we put these back on the tree."

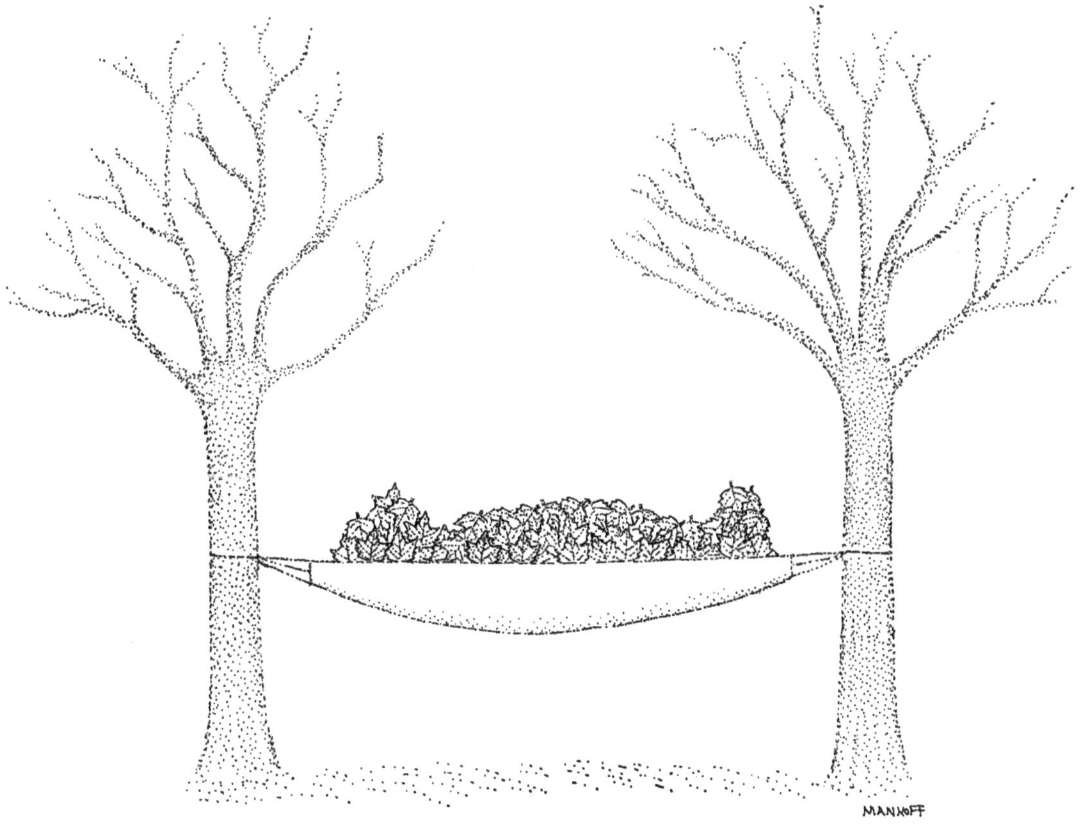
MANKOFF

"Good morning. Fen, Boscage, Bracken & Spinney."

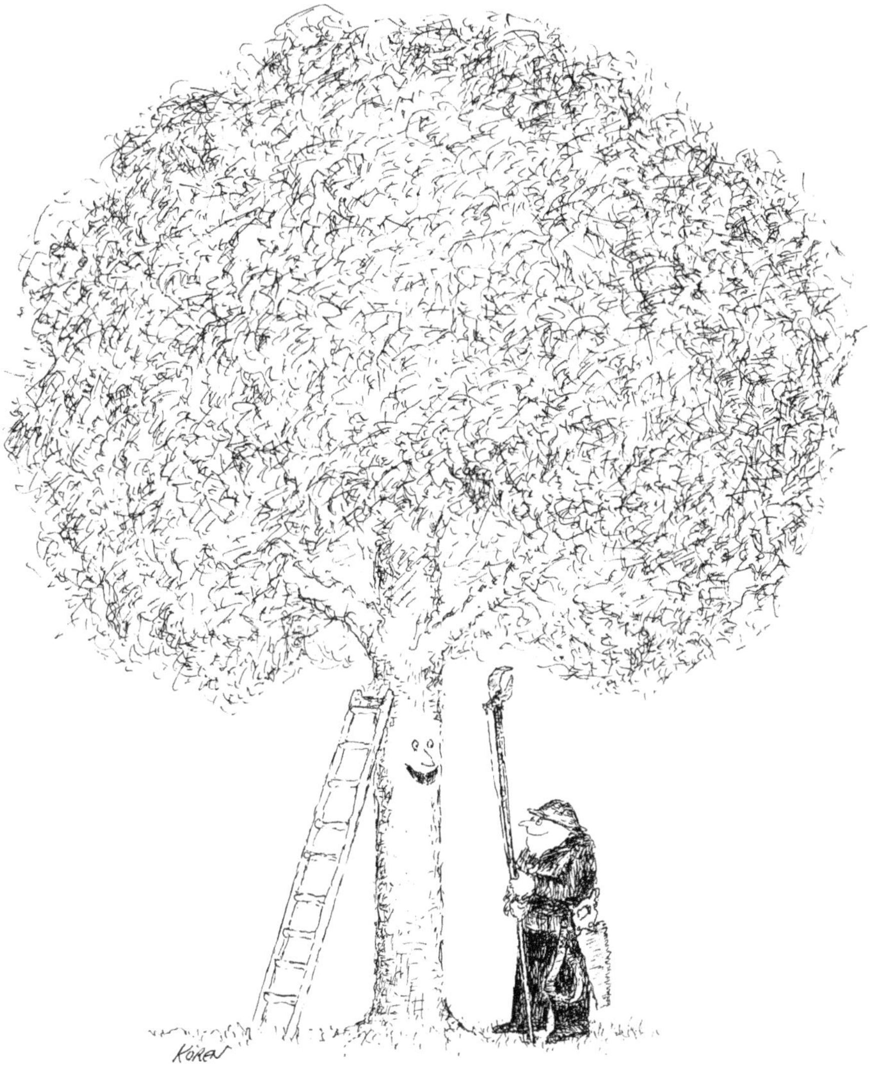
KOREN

"Just a little off the top and shape the back."

THE PHANTOM OF THE GARDEN

C Barsotti

"Oh, Lord! Here comes that common garden pest again!"

MYRA'S LITTLE GARDEN

The corn was as low
As an elephant's toe.

R. Chast

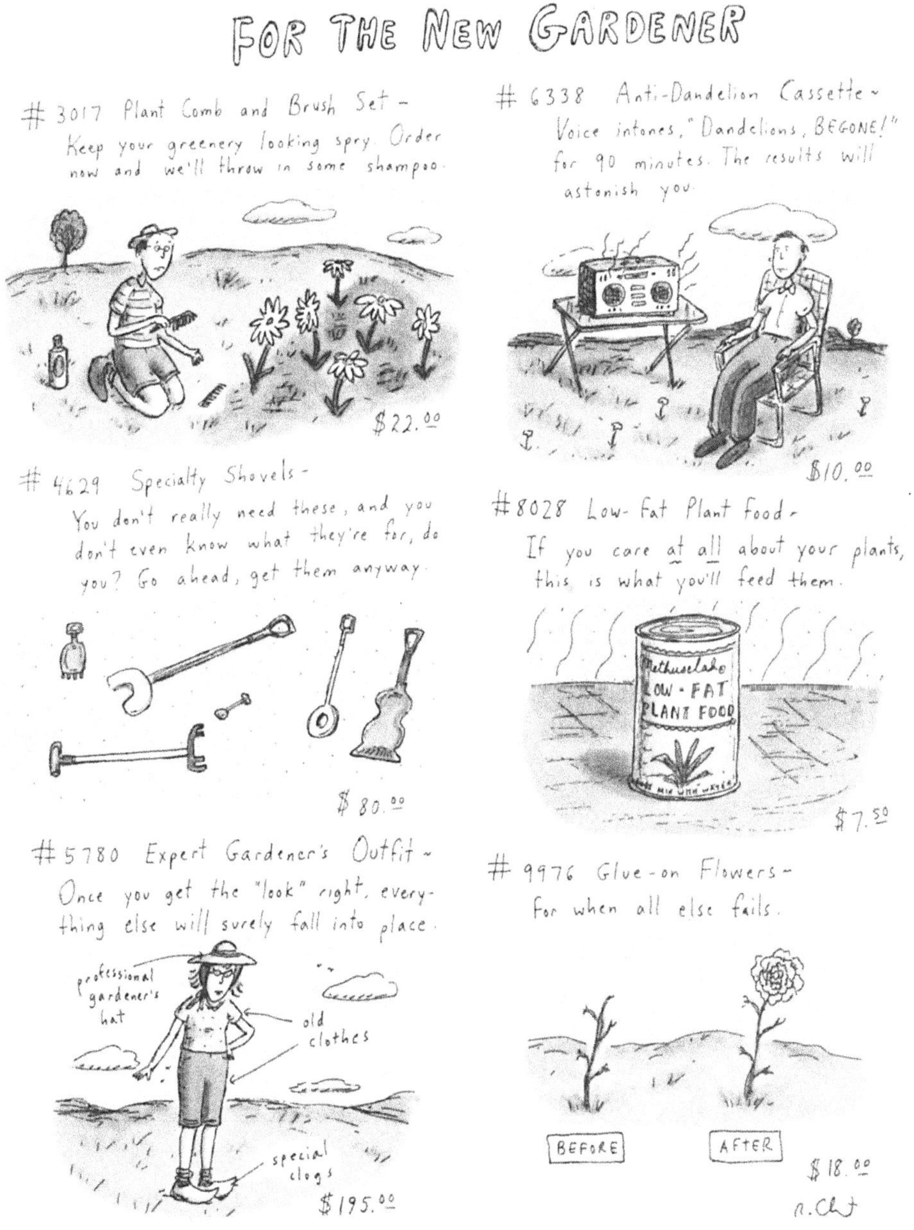

FOR THE NEW GARDENER
#3017 Plant Comb and Brush Set -
Keep your greenery looking spry. Order now and we'll throw in some shampoo.
$22.00
#4629 Specialty Shovels -
You don't really need these, and you don't even know what they're for, do you? Go ahead, get them anyway.
$80.00
#5780 Expert Gardener's Outfit -
Once you get the "look" right, everything else will surely fall into place.
professional gardener's hat
old clothes
special clogs
$195.00
#6338 Anti-Dandelion Cassette -
Voice intones, "Dandelions, BEGONE!" for 90 minutes. The results will astonish you.
$10.00
#8028 Low-Fat Plant Food -
If you care at all about your plants, this is what you'll feed them.
Methuselah
LOW-FAT
PLANT FOOD
$7.50
#9976 Glue-on Flowers -
For when all else fails.
BEFORE
AFTER
$18.00

OUR PRIVACY POLICY
HAS CHANGED.
HA

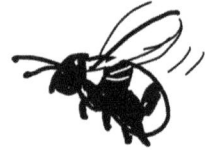

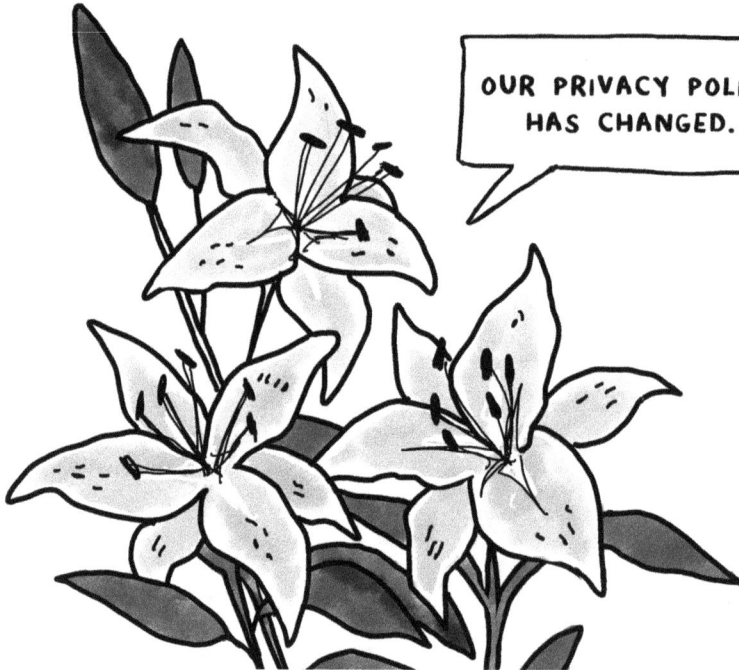

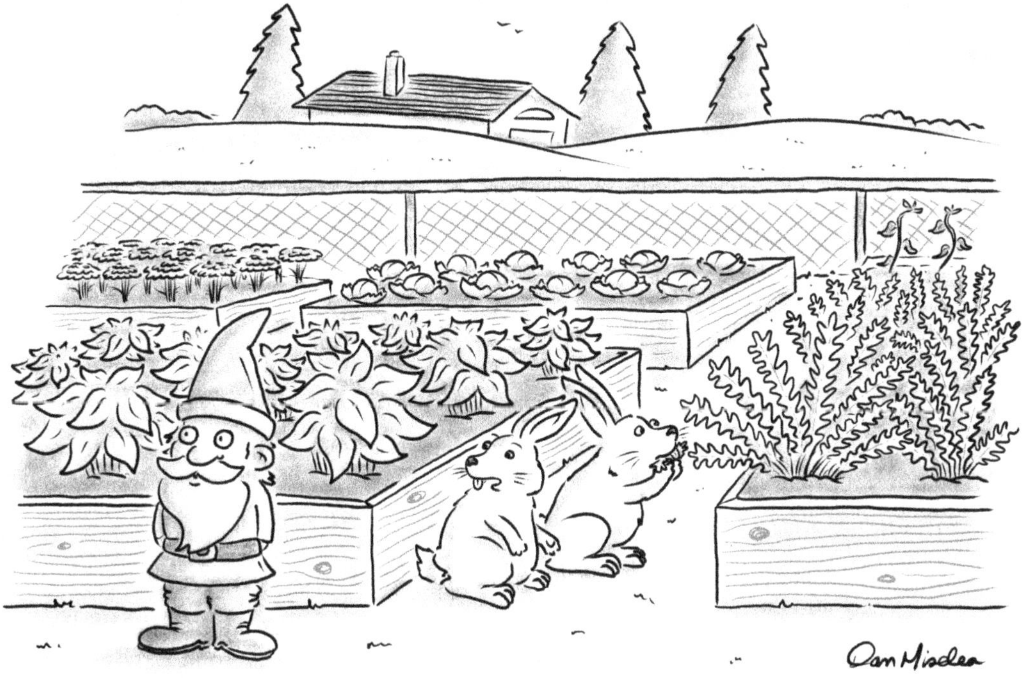
Dan Misdea

"Can you believe we walked right past security?"

Index of Artists

www.ingramcontent.com/pod-product-compliance
Lightning Source LLC
Chambersburg PA
CBHW060759150426
42813CB00058B/2735